HOW TO
WRITE
LETTERS
THAT
SELL

**Other books by Christian H. Godefroy,
also published by Piatkus**

The Complete Time Management System
(with John Clark)

*The Outstanding Negotiator: How to develop
your arguing power* (with Luis Robert)

*Confident Speaking: How to communicate
effectively using the Power Talk System*
(with Stephanie Barrat)

*Mind Power: Use positive thinking to change
your life* (with D.R. Steevens)

*Super Health: How to control your body's
natural defences*

How to
WRITE LETTERS THAT SELL

CHRISTIAN H. GODEFROY
& DOMINIQUE GLOCHEUX

PIATKUS

The author and publishers would like to thank the following companies for permission to reproduce material on pages 20–23: Actionaid, Brann Direct Marketing, British Heart Foundation, Nightingale Conant, and the Royal Society for the Prevention of Cruelty to Animals.

First published in Great Britain in 1994 by
Judy Piatkus (Publishers) Ltd, 5 Windmill Street, London W1P 1HF

First paperback edition, 1995

The moral right of the author has been asserted

A catalogue record of this book is available from the British Library

ISBN 0 7499 1179 4 hbk
ISBN 0 7499 1413 0 pbk

Edited by Carol Franklin
Designed by Paul Saunders
Typeset by Phoenix Photosetting, Chatham, Kent
Printed and bound in Great Britain by
Mackays of Chatham PLC, Chatham, Kent

To André Bideaud, my first master in copywriting, and to Gene Schwartz, whose talent and creativity enlighten my copy and show me The Way.

Contents

Foreword

What separates a 'great' writer from a 'good' writer?

Their focus.

'Good' writers get caught in the trap of focusing on what they're selling. They fool themselves into thinking that if they can describe the product or service in irresistible terms, the reader will want it.

'Great' writers go one step beyond. Instead of focusing on what's being sold, they focus on the reader – or, more specifically – the reader's heart. The reader's heart is the door to their wallet. Open their heart and you'll open their wallet.

Are you going to be a 'good' writer and settle for describing things well – or a 'great' writer and open the heart of your reader?

The shelves of the bookshops are flooded with books that teach you how to be a 'good' writer. This book is different. It reveals the secrets of how to be a 'great' writer.

The decision is yours.

Ted Kikoler
Mail order designer
and graphic consultant

Introduction

Generate thousands of pounds' worth of sales right from your own home

In the beginning, everyone made fun of me. Work for myself? Too risky. No one believed I could do it.

> 'Well, I found THE WAY. I'm through with working for other people. I do what I like . . . when I like. And my bank account keeps growing and growing.'

Last year, I marketed my products to more than 200,000 people in over 18,000 towns and cities. You can do the same, I'll tell you how

- with no travelling or hotel expenses;
- with no stress or fatigue;
- with no salespeople and no waste of time.

I stay at home. I have a few employees. I live quietly in my village. I can see the trees and the fields from my window. What a life!

How did I do it? I used a new technique. I learned how to write letters that are so attractive and so convincing, that someone 1,000 miles away wants to send me a cheque and get my merchandise.

And now here is a formula which will enable anyone – including you – to do the same thing. Interested? Read on . . .

A former distributor of business correspondence told me his secrets, all the 'tricks of the trade' I needed to push my sales figures sky high. Since then,

I've discovered my own techniques. I put them all together and came up with an infallible 'formula'.

In the last seven years, I've written all kinds of letters: sales letters; business letters; administrative memos; even legal letters. Everything a salesperson can do, I now do by letter. And it always works!

Why?

Because each letter is tried and tested. The impact of each sentence has been planned. I don't have any theories, any opinions or personal preferences. Sales figures and profits are my only judge.

Being very enthusiastic about my success, I revealed my 'formula' to a few friends. These are the astonishing results.

- A publisher friend doubled his subscriptions.

- Another multiplied his sales by seven.

- A third, who was selling trucks for a large dealership, learned how to write letters. He now has his own business, and earns three times as much money as before.

- Yet another, in the electronic equipment field, multiplied his sales three times and is now showing a healthy profit.

Then the idea came to me: make my formula available to others, by writing a 'method'.

Fait accompli. My method is called *How to write letters that sell*.

This book contains all the sample letters, checklists, secrets and techniques that have worked for me. I've kept nothing back. It's all here.

Why did I decide to give all this away? Because I want to give you the same helping hand that someone gave me a few years ago. Someone who put me on the road to success. It's only right to give, after getting so much.

Whether you're a businessman or woman, a shopkeeper, a salesperson, or just young and ambitious, with a desire to succeed – if you write one letter a day or 100 a month – this method will lead you to success.

Christian H Godefroy
January 1994

CHAPTER 1

How a simple letter can make people open their wallets

Think of a situation when you have to convince someone to do something for you. It's important. You have to be at your most persuasive. You may not get a second chance. For example:

- You have to convince your bank manager to do you a favour or allow you more credit.

- You want to get a very good deal on a car.

- You're the head of an organisation, or an elected official, and you have to raise funds for an important project.

- You've got your eye on a flat and you want the landlord to lower the price.

- You're trying to get the Inland Revenue to grant you a substantial reduction.

- You want your major supplier to agree to more favourable terms of payment.

- You want to convince your housing association to install a lift in your building.

- You want to gain the romantic affection of a man or woman.

- You know you have a great product and you want to reach the largest number of potential buyers.

There are many approaches and techniques at your disposal for convincing all these people. But the one we're about to show you has four incomparable advantages over all the others.

1

1. You can use it in practically any situation.

2. This method can be used as a complement to any other technique. For example, it can serve as added leverage to any ongoing negotiations, or in your campaign to persuade people.

3. It is effective over long distances: there is no need for you to go anywhere. This makes it VERY economical and VERY easy to do.

4. You don't need a charismatic personality, or nerves of steel, or a poker player's ability to bluff opponents out. If you're a shy person, or if you have trouble expressing yourself in front of other people, you can still use this method as effectively as Lee Iacocca or the president of the United States!

This method, which allows you to sell, negotiate, convince people and obtain what you want, faster and more easily than you thought possible (from family, friends, suppliers, tax inspectors, judges, your boss, sales reps of all kinds etc.), was originally developed by some of the great names in advertising: names like Ogilvy, Hopkins and Caples. Add to these the knowledge and expertise of specialists in human psychology and psycho-sociology, and years of research, experiments and on-site testing costing millions of pounds, and you have the most effective, sane and gentle means of persuasion available to anyone, anywhere in the world.

We're not going to try to teach you how to manipulate people and get them to do things against their will. Not at all. On the contrary, what we're trying to do is teach you how to *understand* people better, and also how to *like* people more, so that you can offer them a valuable service, be of use to them AND attain your own objectives, all at the same time. You can do all this, even though your personal objectives are very, very ambitious.

So what's the method called? It's called **copywriting**.

That's right – copywriting, which literally means writing a model text that is subsequently copied. Because, very often, original texts are brought up to date, improved, adjusted etc. Or if they don't need to be updated, only the 'key' (discussed in detail later on) may have to be changed.

Becoming a millionaire in 20 steps

Perhaps becoming a millionaire isn't one of your priorities for the coming months and years. But surely you would be interested in finding out about a way to earn more money, *a lot more money*, starting today.'

Imagine all the things you could do if you had more money at your disposal: buy a bigger house or a new car; take exotic holidays; go out more often; help your friends; give more to charity etc. You'd be able to make all the things you've been dreaming about come true. You'd experience that calm sense of assurance that financially comfortable people feel: a sense of complete security about the future and total confidence in themselves.

What can you do to earn all this money? Well, I'm going to show you a simple process that can make you a millionaire. After that, it's up to you to set your own limits: £50,000, £100,000, £750,000, £1,000,000 – it's totally up to you! Later on we'll take a look at the advantages and the risks of this method. And also at ways to limit those risks and obtain maximum benefits.

Ready? Imagine that you've written a direct mail letter which brings you a return of £2 for every £1 you invest. Starting with only £1, you'd have to reinvest your earnings only 20 times in order to make a million pounds. Sounds too good to be true? Well, here's the proof:

1st time	£	2	5
2nd	£	4	10
3rd	£	8	20
4th	£	16	40
5th	£	32	80
6th	£	64	160
7th	£	128	320
8th	£	256	640
9th	£	512	1,280
10th	£	1,024	2,560
11th	£	2,048	5,120
12th	£	4,096	10,240
13th	£	8,192	20,480
14th	£	16,384	40,960
15th	£	32,768	81,920
16th	£	65,536	163,840
17th	£	131,072	327,680
18th	£	262,144	655,360
19th	£	524,288	1,310,720
20th	£1,048,576		2,621,440

'But,' you may object, 'at the rate of one mailing a month, using the same letter 20 times would take over a year and a half.'

Well, there's nothing to prevent you, commercially, legally or financially speaking, from sending out a mailing once a week. At that rate, it would only take you five months to make your first million.

Also, you're not obliged to invest only £1 at the start. If your initial investment is £5, you'd only need 19 mailings to reach your goal.

It's always technically and financially better to send out the largest number of letters you can: doing this substantially improves the cost/return ratio for each letter sent (we'll be talking more about this later on).

Is there a limit to how large mailings should be?

The answer to this question is simple: make them as large as the risk you wish to take. You can make a precise calculation of this limit by:

- using tests based on statistics and probability factors that help you predict the results of your mailings in advance (described in detail later on);

- calculating the costs of the mailing (suppliers, printers, delivery service etc.).

But there's more to it than that. What if some letters return three or four or five or six times your initial investment, instead of just twice as much? In many cases the returns are much higher and your chances of multiplying your stake improve as you become more proficient at writing copy.

What if you don't have any money to invest?

'I'm broke . . .'

No problem. Apart from the postal charges, which always have to be paid up front, the other costs (delivery, paper, printing, warehouse space etc.) do not have to be paid in advance. All these costs can be billed *on credit*.

Here's a little secret.

Selling by direct mail is just a game, where you can earn colossal sums . . . mostly by investing other people's money!

The same goes for the stock market, except that stocks are more risky. With direct mail, results are a lot easier to predict, and the success or failure of a campaign depends, to a much greater extent, on you and you alone.

The art of direct-mail sales is a game where hundreds of millions of pounds are placed on the table each and every day.

Are you a player?

Maybe you like winning, like I do? In this book I'm going to tell you about my techniques as a professional player and I'm even going to let you in on a few handy tricks to make sure you come out a winner (all perfectly honest, of course!).

If you're serious about making money from direct mail then mastering the art of copywriting is essential. You'll have to sweat a little, you may have doubts at some point, you may even get discouraged. But, stick it out, and you'll be sure to experience the exaltation and excitement of success, and the joys of being rich.

Basic principles for a successful mailing

What elements are necessary for a successful mailing?

Outer envelope

This is the single most important element. If it isn't opened, nothing happens. There are, of course, the traditional techniques of putting 'PER-SONAL' or 'SPECIAL OFFER' or 'RESERVED FOR ADDRESSEE ONLY' on the envelope. But you can also use the envelope to state clearly what your offer is about, as long as you *arouse the reader's curiosity*. (For more, see chapter 12.)

Sales letter

This is the second most important element. It is a personal message which makes the reader want to buy (your product or service), and strengthens their conviction to do so. We'll have a lot more to say about it later on.

Brochure

Whatever the letter cannot do must be done by the enclosed brochure: its design, pictures, diagrams, endorsements etc.

Order form

The simpler it is, and the easier to fill out, the better. Keep the sales message clear: the idea is to be able to convince someone by getting them to read only the order form.

Reply envelope

Always include one in your package. You mustn't expect a potential client to find their own envelope – doing so could very well lose you the sale, since the client will probably put off replying (or forget about it completely) because they haven't got an envelope handy.

In direct mail sales *later means never*.

Support letter

Included in this category are any documents that can help sales, such as testimonials from satisfied clients. Adding them to your mailing or not may depend on the weight of your package: post offices usually set certain weight limits and surpassing them by even a fraction of an ounce can double the cost of your mailing.

Provide a return guarantee

A study was conducted in Germany which showed that over 500 mail order firms in that country were 'fly by night' operations, i.e. they accepted orders from clients but never delivered the goods. For a while these kinds of despicable operators were threatening the entire mail order industry's survival. Despite stringent laws and constant surveillance by consumer protection groups, people still need to be reassured that your mail order offer is 'on the level'.

Do anything you can do to reassure them. A return guarantee is indispensable if you want to establish a positive and honest relationship with your clients.

Because when you think about it, what do consumers really have to base their decisions on? Promises, maybe a retouched photograph or a pretty drawing. What they don't have in front of them is the product itself. So, to avoid mistrust and resentment, promise people a prompt and full refund if they are not satisfied. This will also protect you against any legal problems with consumer associations and protection groups.

Give your letter a personal look

Print it up in different colours, use a friendly 'typewritten' typeface or type it on a typewriter instead of having it typeset. Sign the letter and use a different colour for the signature than for the rest of the text. Choose a textured paper that looks more like paper you'd buy to write a letter to someone or print a subtle grain on to the paper.

The more your letter looks handwritten, and destined for a single person, the better your sales will be.

Pay special attention to the text of your letter

The major portion of this book is devoted to this subject, and this subject alone. It is the most important part of making your mailing campaign a success. Nothing will happen if your letter isn't well written. You can have the best product in the world, you may be offering a fantastic price, but if your message doesn't respect the rules of direct mail copywriting, then you'll invariably lose money.

Good copywriting can double your sales and even multiply them ten times over. Similarly, your profits will increase 100 per cent to 1,000 per cent. An added response of only 0.2 per cent can double your profits in some cases. Therefore, anything you can do to increase your responses, even things which may seem trivial, are worth the effort. A leverage effect comes into play, which can increase profits 10, 20, 50, 100 per cent and even more!

A good sales letter (and this is very important to understand) can result in *a considerable increase in profit*. To prove the validity of what I'm saying, take a look at this study, conducted by an American company. The same target group was sent five different mailings:

1. A 'self-mailer' (including sales letter, order form and return envelope in the same document);

2. a brochure;

3. a brochure combined with a letter, printed on the first page of the brochure;

4. a very extensive brochure, accompanied by a short letter;

5. a great sales letter accompanied by a very small brochure.

The results were as follows:

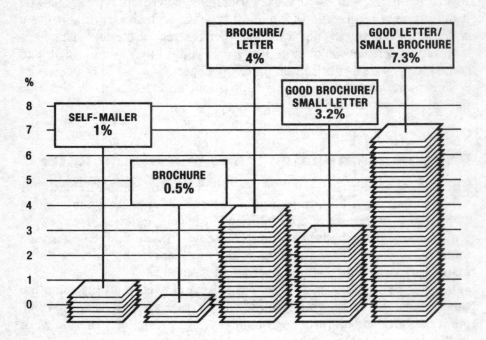

Too often, failure is attributed to factors other than the quality of the writing. Of course, there are limits to what good writing can do. A bad product which is well marketed won't last very long. But a good product which is well marketed – well, that's exactly what empires are built on!

How can you do a good job selling your proposals, your projects, your services or products? The following pages contain all the basic principles, all the fine points and professional tricks of this tried and tested method of effective sales: copywriting.

SUMMARY

Whatever your situation, and whatever initial problems you have to deal with, if you have something specific to ask, either of an individual, or of a large number of individuals, you must know how to make use of the technique of written persuasion: copywriting.

Good copywriting can produce amazing results, especially in the field of mail order marketing, where its impact generates vastly improved sales, to the point where the gross profits of an operation can be doubled, tripled, even multiplied tenfold, because of the leverage effect.

. . . .

CHAPTER 2

An easy way to get large numbers of people to respond to your letter

The entire future of your business depends on this moment . . .

Whether you're looking for a sponsor, a job, clients or investors; whether you sell books, insurance policies, machinery, clothes, property, boats or even yourself . . . any time you have to address people you do not know with the aim of selling something, you always have to establish some kind of 'business relationship'.

What do you think is the most important moment in a business relationship?

The answer is the *very first* moment, i.e. the moment you establish *contact* with a future client.

The entire future of your business depends on this initial contact: either prospective clients let you speak and listen to you, thereby giving you at least a chance to convince them; or they shut the door very quickly and refuse even to consider your offer.

When that happens, even the best products, offered at the best of prices, described in superb catalogues, with excellent samples – are useless. Once a client decides not to listen, the game is over and you might as well pack it up and try somewhere else.

Each time you establish contact with a prospective client, you have a fraction of a second to capture that person's attention.

Read it or throw it away: the decision is made in a fraction of a second

Above all, don't expect a second chance (or a third or fourth): you have to arouse the reader's curiosity and capture his or her attention the very first instant contact is made.

Why? Because people are in a hurry. They have a lot to do and no time to waste. Also, there's a lot of competition out there. Selling by direct mail has become very popular and people often find their letter-boxes stuffed with various amazing offers, which they either read or throw directly into the dustbin.

Result: the time you have to capture your reader's attention is getting shorter and shorter.

It's exactly the same as when someone knocks unexpectedly at your door. You immediately think, 'Is this some kind of scam? Is the person going to try and sell me something? Or ask me to give money to a charity? Is it a friend? Is it the postman with a registered letter?'

If the person is a sales rep, they only have a fraction of a second to get you to listen before you shut the door, saying something like, 'I'm really not interested . . .' or 'I don't need any, thanks . . .'.

The only way to get the odds on your side

Before going any further, I must ask for your complete attention.

The most effective letter, written by the best professional copywriter around, will be useless and do absolutely nothing for you (on the contrary, it will cost you time and money) *if it is not read*!

In fact, every time an initial contact is made, the entire future of your business (at least the future of your mail order business) is at stake. If you hope to go any further, and eventually make a sale, you have to convince people right from the start.

So, you have to concentrate all your efforts and all your energy on this single and unique objective: capture your prospective clients' attention and keep it so that they will read your message. This is the *only way* to get the odds on your side and make your mailing a success.

How to capture your prospects' attention

Why is it, do you think, that the most dynamic companies (and coincidentally the ones that succeed best) invest millions of pounds each year simply attracting people's attention?

The answer is that this is the most important step in marketing: first capture people's attention and leave them with a positive impression.

Only afterwards can you try to sell. Prospective clients must first be made aware of your enterprise, and be ready to take the time and make the effort to read what you have to say.

Furthermore, experience has shown that as far as sales are concerned, first impressions often set the tone for everything that follows. As the saying goes: '**Beware of first impressions – they're usually right!**'

Everything begins at the moment of initial identification.

Try petting a dog without first giving it a chance to sniff you out. You might get your hand bitten!

People aren't much different. No one will feel comfortable engaging in a serious conversation with someone they don't know, especially if the person isn't especially attractive.

How to gain the confidence of prospective clients

With this in mind, take the necessary measures to control the way you look. In the case of direct mail sales, you don't have to dress yourself up in a new suit, but you do have to dress up your mailing, so that people notice you and feel confident about doing business with you.

If you were to meet your prospects in person, you'd do everything you could to look your best, wouldn't you?

There's nothing unusual about that – people don't buy things if they don't have confidence in the salesperson. That's why a female sales rep gets her hair done, and goes out and buys a smart outfit before making an important presentation. A male rep would wear his best suit and tie, make sure he's well groomed etc.

Ask yourself why some people brag about being able to judge others based only on the way they look. It's because we are all inclined, to varying degrees, to do the same thing.

So, to capture your clients' attention, you have to present them with an outward appearance that they can identify immediately, and which makes them want to know more about you, i.e. to listen to you, or read your text, and find out what you expect from them . . .

How to get clients to identify you quickly and easily

This objective is so important, so crucial to the success of your mailing, that we've devoted an entire section to it: 'The secrets of high performance envelopes'.

However, although the envelope stage is extremely important, it isn't enough: once your prospects have opened the envelope, they still have to want to find out more about you. This is achieved by carefully planning the following.

- The contents and arrangement of all documents contained in the envelope. The order in which you place your documents – and therefore the order in which your prospects open them – is very important: *everything* must be done to make reading your message easy and *everything* must be calculated to make them want to find out more. In this way, you lead them towards your final objective, which of course is convincing them to buy. This topic is covered in detail below.

- The contents of your sales letter and especially its heading (covered in detail later on), since this document is the most important follow-up (in the process of leading your prospects towards the act of buying) to the identification you have worked so hard to establish, in terms of credibility, commercial viability or your product, honesty of your operation etc.

The secret that makes people want to read your message

How can you arouse your prospects' interest, so that they want to read your message and find out more about you? The answer is very simple and 100 per cent effective: talk about them, and their problems, their worries, their cares, their hopes and desires. This is an infallible way to get people interested in what you have to say and what you want them to do (buy your product or service).

I say 'talk' because before you write anything down, you start by talking to the people you want to reach in your mind. Writing is just a matter of transcribing what you would say to someone in person – at least that's the way it is in copywriting.

This method has been used since ancient times, even by great philosophers like Socrates and Plato, and it has always been extremely effective. It is still the most effective way of attracting someone's attention, sympathy and in some cases even love!

Yet the technique is really so simple.

How can you make it work for you?

Three types of mail – and the one to avoid

Your prospective client has just emptied his or her letter-box and is about to sort through the mail.

Imagine yourself, early in the morning, picking up your post. Close your eyes for a moment and visualise the scene . . .

At first glance, there are three types of mail. This is sorted according to the type of document contained in the envelope. See opposite.

These categories can be further divided into two main types.

1. *Impersonal mail*, which is printed up in bulk, and sent to thousands of households. This includes publicity, bank statements, bills, public notices etc. Among these documents, some interest us (tax returns, bank statements, publicity about a product we need etc.), while most do not interest us.

2. *Personal letters*. What makes a letter personal? The way it is written, of course. You take a pen and paper, or a typewriter, and you start talking to the person to whom you are writing.

Even in the personal category, there are some letters which contain news or valuable information, and which are interesting, and others which contain nothing of interest.

Initial conclusions from this are:

1. make your letter look as personal as possible;

2. arouse the reader's interest as quickly as possible.

How to personalise your letter

It is almost as important to know what you should *not* do, as what you should do to succeed. Think about it for a moment: if you want your letter to look personal, what should you avoid?

Write down your answers here (give precise examples):

_____

_____

_____

_____

One of the most common faults is to have your letter boringly typeset. The second is not to include a signature. (Do you ever write letters and then not

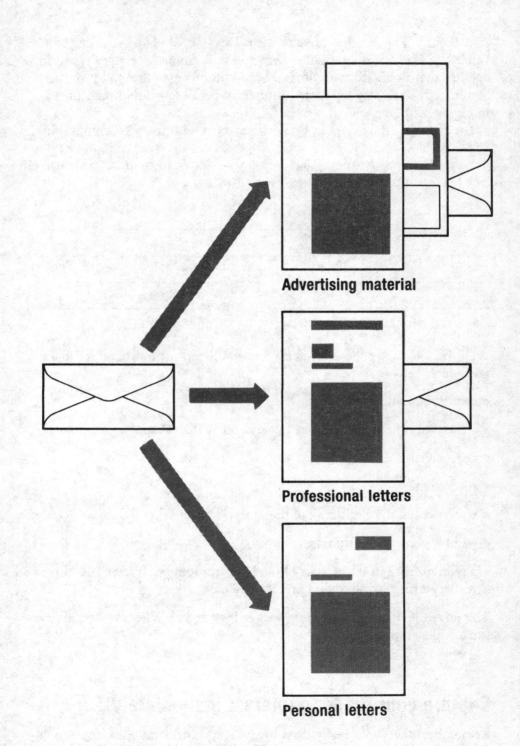

Advertising material

Professional letters

Personal letters

The three types of mail.

sign them?) The third is to start with 'Dear Sir/Madam . . .' or 'Dear Client . . .' which is a bit better, but still bad. Some letters are typed in colours that don't exist on normal typewriters, some are badly printed or blurred, some use too many different typefaces, or too much underlining or bold face, etc.

On the next few pages, you'll find some examples of things you shouldn't do.

Now what about things that make your letter look more personal? Try to come up with a few ideas yourself:

_____

_____

_____

_____

We'll be looking at these elements in detail later on, but here are just a few which help:

- clear typewritten characters;

- a signature that looks real, in a colour other than that of the text itself;

- personalised text (style);

- recent date;

- references at the beginning of the letter;

- handwritten word or phrase;

- a reference, right at the start of the letter, to some characteristic of the reader, which involves him or her personally.

The envelope is also important: does it look right? Whenever possible, use a real stamp.

Capture your reader's interest immediately!

Remember that you really have very, very little time to capture a reader's interest. An average of five to ten per cent of people immediately throw all the direct mail envelopes they receive away, without even opening them, never mind reading them.

Eighty per cent of people allow an average of 20 seconds per envelope, before making a decision either to throw it away, or adopt what is called a 'pre-sales attitude', which means that they are sufficiently interested to want to know more about the product, its price, its capabilities etc.

(The final ten per cent of people regularly read their direct mail.)

These figures are based on scientific research conducted by direct marketing agencies, using high speed cameras, chronometers and special tape recorders that enable them to accurately observe the process which takes place when people receive direct mail.

If you could sit in on some of their working sessions, you'd be in for a few surprises. For example, do you think people read your documents line by line, in the order in which they're written? Not at all. On the contrary, you'd think from observing the way people open and read mail that there wasn't any order or rationale to their reading at all! But this is only an initial impression – the reality is quite different . . .

Researchers have discovered the following.

1. Depending on the type of message and the target audience, an average of 90 per cent of people take eight to twelve seconds to open the envelope and unfold the contents enough to begin reading.

2. The next phase (approach and discovery) also takes place very rapidly: again an average of between eight to twelve seconds, during which time prospects move from one document to another, finally returning to the sales letter, where they select certain bits of information. At the end of this phase (on average 20 seconds after finding the envelope in their letter-box), your prospects reach a fork in the road: either they throw the whole thing away (or put off reading it for later) on they continue reading with growing interest. This is called 'second phase' reading.

3. During second phase reading, prospects examine each element in detail. And in 85 per cent of cases, this phase automatically begins with the sales letter. The human eye usually looks at the upper right-hand part of the page first. Then it moves over to the left and makes a rapid scan of the page, picking out any text you have emphasised (using bold type, underlining, capitals etc.). Only after this scan is completed does the actual reading (or, to be more accurate, survey-ing) begin.

So, to capture your reader's interest in the first few seconds, you must make the most you can of the two main areas of the page, marked numbers 1 and 2 on the diagram below.

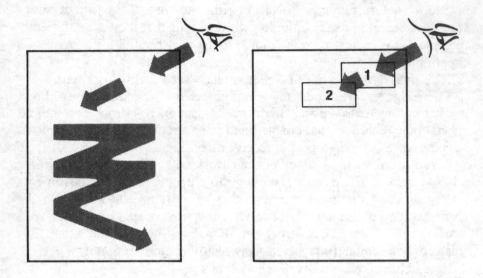

Imagine your prospective clients receiving your letter. They open the outer envelope, take everything out and are immediately confronted with your sales letter (everything has been specially folded so that this objective is achieved). More precisely, they find themselves looking at the upper third part of the sales letter.

If that portion of the page triggers a positive response in your clients' minds, they'll open the letter and start reading. Remember that whenever people are presented with a sales letter, their attention is automatically and unconsciously attracted to the upper third portion of the page.

And research has shown, among other things, that the human eye is first attracted to the upper right-hand corner of the page (why this is so is open to conjecture: is it because we read from left to right, so that for us the left signifies the past, and right the future? If this is true, then people reading Arabic, from right to left, would do the exact opposite . . .).

The same studies have also shown that the first thing 85 per cent of people read is the letter's 'heading' or letterhead (if there is one). This is where you'd place:

■ your company's logo;

■ your company's name, address, telephone and fax numbers.

Four objectives of your letterheading

If you plan to add a heading to your sales letter, make sure it achieves the following four objectives.

- That it attracts your prospects' visual interest.

- That it makes it easy for prospects to identify your company.

- That it makes reading easy (which means the text should be short, reduced to bare essentials, written in simple language and devoid of any references to financial solvency, legalities, etc.).

- That it makes moving on to the next paragraph easy and natural (ideally, the last character in your letterhead will be on the same vertical plane as the first letter of the next paragraph).

Should you use a letterhead or make your letter anonymous?

Question: Should you use a letterhead at all?

If your company's letterhead serves to *reinforce* your message, then the answer is yes. If not, then don't include one, and use the privileged, upper right-hand position for something else (we'll tell you what later on). Put your address somewhere else (see page 25). This will give your letter a much better chance of being perceived as personal.

Here are a few examples of letterheads and layouts:

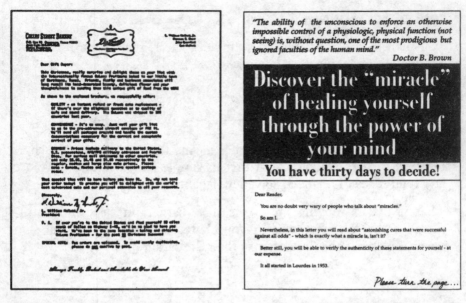

This letter sells cakes. The letterhead and motif suggest a sense of tradition and craftsmanship.

A strong heading and a quote from a doctor catch the eye and make you read on. The letter is structured in such a way that you are persuaded to turn the page.

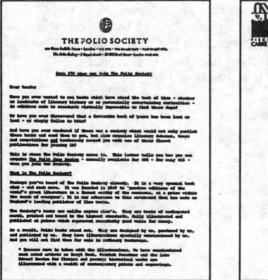

This letter is selling literary classics. The typeface used for the letterhead is suitably classic and elegant. Note the logo, done in calligraphy.

This letter is promoting swimming pools. The illustrated letterhead reinforces the message, for those people who respond more strongly to visual images.

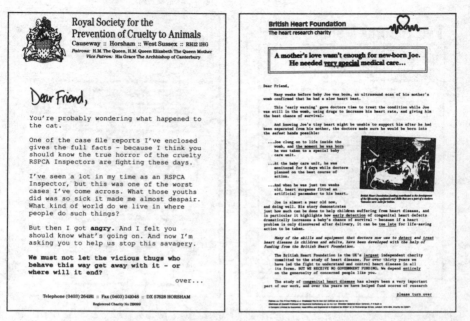

The contrast between the very official-looking letterhead and the handwritten 'Dear Friend' is attractive and makes you want to read on.

The design of this letterhead shows the logo of an electro-cardiogram, which suggests matters of life or death. The headline is far more prominent than the letterhead and grabs the reader's attention.

If your letterhead is well-known, there is always a risk of boredom, which is fatal. Here, the headline and card bring the letter to life.

This sober, elegant letterhead helps to promote the letter's text. It suggests a classic and up-to-date company.

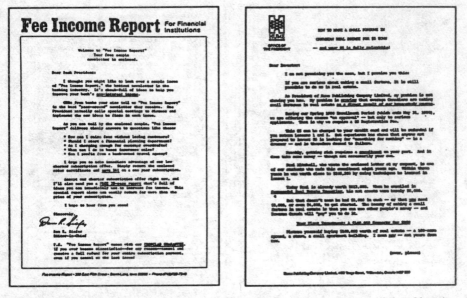

The frame draws attention to the text of this business letter.

Here, the logo is at the top and the address is at the bottom. The chosen typeface, Times, is reassuringly businesslike.

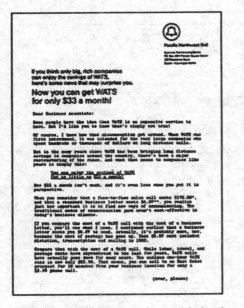

The logo and address are in the top right-hand corner, in the same typeface as the headline: Univers, one of the classic business typefaces.

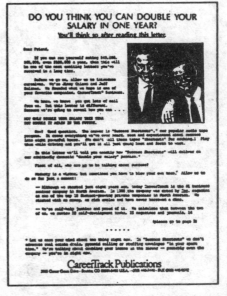

Here, the headline at the top of the page immediately hooks the reader. The letterhead, in a modern typeface, is at the bottom. The photograph makes the letter more personal and approachable.

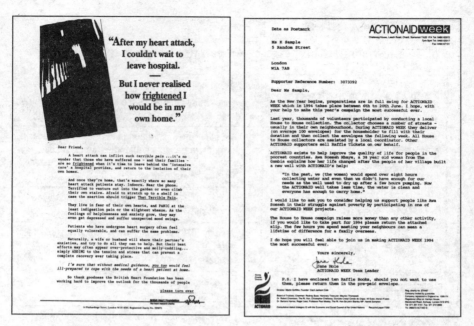

A photograph can dramatize a personal message. This heading gives the impression of a personal encounter with the author. Here, the letterhead is at the foot.

If you want to give an impression of seriousness, use a serious font. This one, a classic Helvetica Light, inspires trust and professionalism.

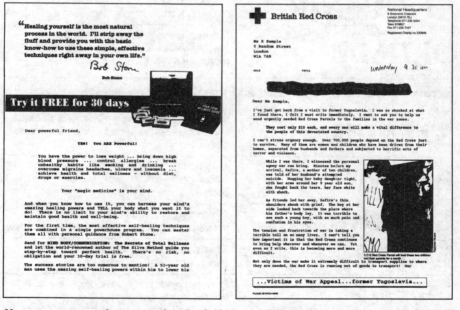
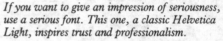

You can use your product *as your letterhead, if it is attractive. Here, the combination of the offer, 'Try it free for 30 days' and the picture of the product catch the reader's attention.*

A well-known symbol gives an instant message to the reader.

Useful typefaces

Here are a few standard typefaces you can use for your letterheads:

HELVETICA	One of the most widely used typefaces. Its clean lines inspire confidence (honesty) and modernity (industry).
TIMES	The other, most common (and classic) typeface. It has a more traditional, old-style look and adds weight to your text (often used in areas of finance, banking, investment etc.).
Script	An elegant, rather feminine typeface, often used for invitations, decoration etc.
BODONI	Used by IBM as its standard typeface, it evokes a sense of solidity and continuity (computers, business texts etc.).
Futura	The same style as Helvetica, but a little less intimidating (commercial).
Avant-Garde	A very 'designed' typeface, attractive and modern (architecture – design).
GARAMOND	A very elegant, old-fashioned typeface, often used in literature (publishing, printing etc.).
SOUVENIR	This typeface evokes the turn of the century (antiques, furniture, interior decoration etc.).
OPTIMA	A modern and very simple typeface, used by medical publications, and in laboratory and technological information, etc.

Here are a few more specialised and imaginative typefaces:

STENCIL	Suggests a rustic atmosphere and materials like wood and leather (construction, hardware, wood products etc.).
Bembo	And old typeface suggesting days gone by (restaurants, hotels, antiques, antiquarian booksellers).
Broadway	This typeface suggests leisure and celebration (restaurants, nightclubs, theatres and concert halls).
MACHINE	A heavy typeface which lives up to its name (garages, heavy industries etc.).
Vivaldi	An elegant typeface with something of the Italian Baroque (music, arts, classical theatre, etc.).
Korinna	An original typeface which is both square and rounded (printing, arts and crafts, education).

Do letterheadings always act as a reinforcement?

A letterhead can act as a reinforcement in two ways.

First, your prospect already knows about your company and the kind of products you offer. Here your letterhead allows the prospect to identify who you are immediately. If this is not the first time that you've sent the prospect a letter, it means that they have shown an interest in your products in the past, and are therefore likely to want to know more about the product or service you are currently offering. In such cases, a letterhead is absolutely essential.

Secondly, you have a high-end or expensive product which needs to be sold by a company which fits into a certain tradition of respectability (for example, luxury items, collectors' items, antiques, cultural artefacts like Aboriginal paintings, and even certain financial products like insurance policies and investment portfolios – all these require the extra assurance of 'respectability' and 'credibility' associated with tradition). In such cases:

- use traditional or prestige typefaces;

- the name of the company should evoke a sense of tradition or history, a well-known region, an era, a country;

- your logo and/or heading should be subtle and in good taste.

In all other cases, it is better to reduce the letterhead to its bare minimum, so as not to interfere with the rest of the text. You can even leave it out completely and make full use of the top part of the page to capture your reader's interest.

In any case, if your prospects really want to know who you are, i.e. who wrote the letter, all they have to do is:

- look at the bottom of the first page, where you will have printed your company's name, address, phone and fax number; or

- turn to the end of the letter, where they'll find your signature, followed by your name and title, and the company's address.

How can you make optimum use of this *very* important part of the page (upper right-hand corner)?

This part of the page corresponds to the hook on a fisherman's line. And one of the major discoveries of copywriting is this: place the most attractive bait you can find on your hook. Professional copy writers call this bait simply: the HOOK or HEADLINE.

The doorway to your letter: how to make it open automatically for prospective clients

The headline

The doorway to your letter is its headline. It is the key factor to making your mailing a success.

> 'Day-to-day hassles (Did I remember to take my wallet? Did I lock the back door . . .) Worries . . . holiday plans . . . children . . . money problems . . . a bit of good news . . . bad news . . . the car broke down . . . don't forget to call Mother . . . Hurry up or I'll be late . . . Where did I leave my keys . . .? etc. etc.'

Your prospective clients are almost continually thinking about something. An endless stream of thoughts flows through their minds, thoughts which concern and interest them in a very personal way. And they never stop! There's always a backlog of other thoughts trying to push their way in. People's minds are rarely empty – there are always hundreds of thoughts and ideas just waiting to jump in and fill any empty spaces.

What you need to do is stop this continuous flow of thoughts, so that your prospects pay attention to you. All you need is a fraction of a second, after which they'll stop following their own train of thought and start listening to yours. And this stop has to be strong enough to retain their interest right up to the moment of buying.

This is not an easy thing to do . . .

How to get your text read from beginning to end

This is far more difficult and ambitious than simply trying to attract attention!

Not only do you want to attract attention, you also want to capture and retain it, so that your prospects read your message right through to the end, are convinced that they want your product or service, and place their orders . . .

If you had a shop, you wouldn't just want to attract people to look at your window. That would be easy – just put a couple of Belisha beacons outside the shop, make some noise and you'll soon have a crowd of people flocking to see what's going on. But the chances are, as soon as they find out, they'll leave. What you want is for these people to come into your shop – you want to 'hook' them with your headline, so that they are interested enough in your product to take the time and make the effort to find out more about it.

The headline is the hook, which stops their normal flow of thoughts. To show you just how important a good headline is – in fact it can make all the difference between success and failure – take a look at another direct marketing technique: newspaper ads. You've seen those advertising supplements which are often slipped into your newspaper, especially the weekend editions . . . A few years ago, a study was conducted which showed that close to 80 per cent of such supplements, which were aimed specifically at women, were not even noticed by men! Need I say more . . .

Start with a promise

What elements constitute a good headline?
The headline is:

- a sentence or a phrase,

- placed at the head of the text (like the title of a book, chapter or article),

- designed and laid out (using typefaces and colours of your choice) in a way that makes prospects want to continue reading and find out more . . .

- a *promise*.

This last point is extremely important. Remember that word PROMISE. As Samuel Johnson said, 'A promise – a great promise – is the soul of all advertising'.

What are you actually saying when you make a promise? According to the dictionary, a promise 'arouses a sense of probability that a thing or event which is desired will come to pass'. Desire is defined as 'the conscious tension directed at something one wishes to possess'.

The process of making promises is as follows: you formulate words which stimulate your reader's imagination. You promise that one, or a number, of their needs will be satisfied, and they imagine the pleasure they will experience when this takes place.

The basis of all this, as well as the basis of pleasure – and therefore the desire for pleasure – is what are called *needs*.

Next, we will look at how to predict the motives and needs of your target clients, so that you can make promises which result in the greatest number of responses to your offer.

SUMMARY

- The best sales letter in the world accomplishes nothing if it isn't read.

- There is only one way to get prospective clients to read your letter: capture their attention and retain it until they start reading.

- You only have a few seconds to capture your prospect's attention and only a single opportunity to succeed. No second or third tries here! Therefore you must succeed the first time around.

- To improve your chances of success, you have to gain your prospective clients' confidence the moment they identify who you are (by carefully designing your envelope, logo and letterhead), and arouse their interest as much as possible (by personalising your letter, making it easy to read and follow, and above all by coming up with an effective headline).

. . . .

CHAPTER 3

How to come up with promises that produce the greatest number of replies

Predicting the motives and needs of your target clients

Psycho-sociologists have conclusively established that the source of human behaviour, its roots and motives, can be reduced to a number of fundamental needs, which are specific to each individual.

This means that two individuals, observed in isolation, will not react in the same way to the same event, especially over a long period of time.

This is what makes up each individual's personality. And this is what makes us all unique.

However, these same psycho-sociologists have also been able to identify certain basic tendencies in human beings and they have developed a decoding system which enables them to pinpoint these tendencies more easily. For example, they have shown that it is possible clearly to distinguish a number of categories of needs. And one of these researchers, Abraham Maslow, organised these categories into a pyramidal structure, which has since become famous, and which bears his name: Maslow's pyramid. (See diagram below.)

The basis of all action: five fundamental needs

Why a pyramid? Because Maslow realised that these needs are *progressive*: we move from one category to another, from one level to another, in a progressive way. And before superior needs appear, the inferior needs (those at the base of the pyramid) must first be satisfied.

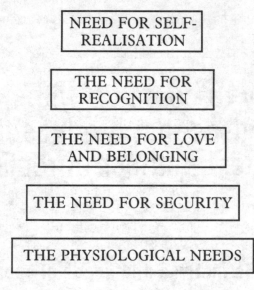

NEED FOR SELF-
REALISATION

THE NEED FOR
RECOGNITION

THE NEED FOR LOVE
AND BELONGING

THE NEED FOR SECURITY

THE PHYSIOLOGICAL NEEDS

Maslow's Pyramid

1. Physiological needs

You leave for a month's holiday in South America. Great! A few days after your arrival, you decide to take a domestic flight in order to explore some of the interior of the country. The small plane takes off. You're flying high over the Andes. It's a majestic sight. Suddenly, there's a shout from the back of the plane. Passengers are getting out of their seats, their faces filled with fear. One of the plane's engines is on fire! Panic spreads. The plane loses altitude, heading straight for the side of a mountain. A few interminable seconds pass . . . and then the crash! You regain consciousness and find yourself among the debris of the aircraft. Miraculously, you are not injured – just a few scratches. But you are the only survivor.

So you start waiting for help to arrive. One hour, two hours, three hours pass, then six, twelve, twenty-four hours. Nothing. One day, two days, three days – still nothing. You've eaten everything you could find in the plane and you've also finished off everything there was to drink. What do you do now?

One point of interest: a few seconds after the crash you found yourself thinking about all kinds of things that are totally different from the things you normally think about. But, 72 hours later, your thoughts have changed once again, and you could say that you're thinking more like a prehistoric cave dweller than like a civilised human being who is rich, healthy and happy . . .

Actually, you're thinking about one thing and one thing only: where to find something to drink. And soon you'll be concentrating all your thoughts on eating, on finding food.

These are what are called physiological needs. They must be satisfied, and the more difficult it becomes to do this, the more ready you are to do 'anything and everything' to satisfy them.

The example above is real enough: it happened to the members of an Argentinian rugby team and their story was even depicted in the film *Alive*. The survivors were forced to turn to cannibalism to survive. Clearly, since they had absolutely nothing else to eat, they decided to consume human flesh rather than die . . .

The same goes for other physiological needs. If you think about your primary, absolutely essential needs, you will come up with a more or less complete list of human beings' physiological needs.

People who have been deprived of the opportunity to fulfil one or another of these physiological needs may suffer for the rest of their lives because of it. Someone who has experienced starvation may build their entire life around this motivating factor: they'll do everything they can to make absolutely certain they never have to undergo the suffering of intense hunger again. It is said, for example, that hunger was the motivating force behind Aristotle Onassis's driving desire to become rich . . .

Now, what does all this have to do with copywriting, you may well ask?

Base your promise on a physiological need

Many promises are partly, or totally, based on these motivating factors. Think about it for a minute and try to make a list of any that come to mind.

- 'Cold? Me? Never!' (ad for thermal clothes)

- 'The thirst-quencher' (Coca-Cola)

- 'My pain disappeared completely' (painkiller)

- 'Eat and drink to your heart's content' (Club Med)

- 'Sleep like a log – without medication' (book on insomnia)

- 'Breathing – so natural, so essential' (air purifier)

Open any magazine or newspaper and you'll find a host of other references to physiological needs.

Now let's get back to our plane crash. You've found enough to drink, and eat, so you aren't hungry or thirsty any more.

So, what new desires do you have now? Well, it's quite simple: you need to feel that your future needs will also be satisfied.

2. Need for security

To return to our example of the plane crash survivor . . . If no help arrives in a few days, you'd start looking for warm clothes, you'd build yourself some kind of shelter to protect yourself from the elements and any dangerous animals, you'd build up a stock of food, you'd look for weapons to hunt and defend yourself, you may even consider cultivating some land so that you will have vegetables to eat later on.

Despite the fact that modern society is pretty well organised in this area (with the availability of social security, unemployment insurance, health care, the police force, and all the other official organisations set up to control and reassure us), it is still possible to observe that the need for security is extremely strong.

You only have to look at the promises made by politicians to realise that the need for security is an extremely powerful motivating factor.

Take a moment to think about all the ad campaigns and publicity headlines which are based on this category of need, and make a list of them.

- 'Our health insurance plan pays you x pounds for every day of work you miss . . .'
- 'Prepare for the unexpected . . .'
- 'Protect your home against theft . . .'
- 'Total road safety and security . . .'
- 'Take charge of your future . . .'

A large part of the things that surround you are the result of your need for security. From your refrigerator to the locks on your doors, from your medicine cabinet to your smoke detectors – you acquire all these things in order to assure your future security.

Some things satisfy both physiological needs and the need for security at the same time.

Whenever emergency situations arise (war, economic depression, crime waves, social upheavals, natural catastrophes etc.), these two levels of need become all the more pressing and demand more than their usual share of attention.

3. Need for love and belonging

You're alone again. Once you get organised so that you don't have to spend too much time worrying about basic needs, you start feeling bored. You have an intense desire for companionship.

After satisfying the first two levels of needs, most people experience a great longing for relations with other people, for love, affection, friendship and companionship. They try to find their place within a group or family unit. Although these needs may have been absent while they were still lacking essentials, they are nevertheless deeply affected by feelings of solitude, rejection, loneliness, rootlessness etc., as well as the lack of tenderness and love.

In life-threatening situations, these feelings are intensified, resulting in feelings of camaraderie among soliders, the 'until death do us part' sentiment central to marriage, the binding force found in street gangs, police forces, terrorist groups etc.

The entire fashion industry, which exploits people's need to feel they belong to a group, is based on the need for love and belonging.

Once again, try to find some examples in the ads you encounter:

- 'You *too* can find love . . .' (dating agency)

- 'The perfect relationship . . .' (dating agency)

- 'How to find someone to love . . .' (book)

- 'How to get rid of your shyness once and for all . . .' (correspondence course)

- 'Public speaking made easy . . .' (book)

- *'How to Win Friends and Influence People . . .'* (a book by Dale Carnegie)

4. Need for recognition

Advertising in general, and direct mail sales in particular, fully exploits the motivating factors resulting from this category of need. We all need to feel that we are of value to ourselves, and we also crave the esteem and recognition of others.

There's nothing harder to accept than being ignored, to the point where people have even been known to commit murder just to get their name in the newspapers so that others notice them!

Who do you think is the most important person in the world to most individuals?

The answer is clear: the most important person in the world to each and every individual is . . . him or herself!

An American telephone company did a study to discover the word that is used most frequently in the English language. The winner, by a wide margin, was the word 'I'.

Remember this, because it's very important: the people you're writing to, even though they may say they are devoted to the well-being of others, and even though they may abhor the word, are first and foremost *egoists*, just like everybody else. They are primarily interested in themselves.

Before going on to the higher levels of needs, attempt the following exercise: sort the following common motivating factors into their respective categories of need – P for physiological; S for security; B for belonging; and R for recognition.

This list is used extensively by copywriters and covers a large portion of the motivating factors used in mail order marketing (a single, motivating factor may fall into more than one category):

Category

1. Earning money ☐

2. Improving health ☐

3. Saving time ☐

4. Being appreciated by others ☐

5. Improving appearance ☐

6. Being fashionable ☐

7. Avoiding criticism ☐

8. Avoiding pain ☐

9. Avoiding losing money ☐

10. Owning beautiful objects ☐

11. Leisure ☐

12. Getting promoted ☐

13. Improving social status ☐

14. Getting compliments ☐

Category

15. Insuring your security and retirement ☐

16. Being more comfortable ☐

17. Attracting the opposite sex ☐

18. Avoiding losing what you possess ☐

19. Avoiding losing your job ☐

20. Avoiding work and/or effort ☐

The answers listed below are not the final word – some factors are obvious, others are open to discussion. Two of the factors do not fit into any of the categories we have discussed so far.

1. S, R	8. P	15. S
2. P	9. S	16. S
3. ?	10. R	17. P, B
4. R	11. ?	18. S
5. B, R	12. R	19. B
6. B, R	13. R	20. P
7. B	14. R	

This leaves us with four examples of physiological needs, five examples of the need for security, five examples of the need for love and belonging, and eight examples of the need for recognition!

5. Need for self-realisation (fulfilment)

Even if all your desires have been satisfied and all your needs fulfilled, you still feel a kind of 'motivational lack' deep in your heart, which forces you to act: this is the need to realise your full potential.

Maslow defined it this way: 'Whatever a person can be, he or she must be.'

This is what makes artists strive to create their masterpieces, or inventors to perfect their ideas, and it's also what makes ordinary people want to improve their lives.

It's very difficult to imagine people who really do fulfil their potential, as long as they are not liberated from the previous levels of need that we all have to deal with.

People often reach this stage in their development only partially, on holiday for example, or during their leisure hours. That's why I would place the motivating factors of 'saving time' and 'having more leisure' in this category.

These needs are not often exploited in direct mail sales because they do not correspond to the needs of the mass market. And, in fact, the higher you climb on the Maslow scale, the fewer people there are at your level.

Other decoding systems

The Maslow scale doesn't explain everything: it's also a good idea, when working on a sales letter, to modify your approach by referring to other decoding systems.

For example, you can use the seven deadly sins.

How to get the most out of the seven deadly sins

Without looking at the list below, try to remember what the seven deadly sins are. If you can't remember one, or more, you might find it interesting to ask yourself why you forgot those sins in particular.

Here is the list:

1. avarice; 5. lust;
2. anger;   6. pride;
3. envy;   7. laziness.
4. gluttony;

The Church did not threaten its followers with fire and brimstone for committing these cardinal sins by accident: the sins represent very strong motivating factors in many men and women.

Today, however, psychologists have shown that by suppressing these motivating factors, the Church caused people serious harm, and even led many believers to develop mental, and especially psychosomatic, illnesses. Suppressed anger is at the root of a number of diseases; a healthy dose of laziness has led to many advances in the human condition; sexuality can be a means of self-fulfilment; pride is sometimes justified; gluttony should be treated as an illness, rather than punished, etc.

Of course I'm not trying to say that lust is a virtue or that avarice is a positive quality!

How to stimulate people's demons in order to sell

Let's be honest: a copywriter who is trying to be an effective salesperson is certain to stimulate one, or a number, of these demons, hidden in the minds of all consumers, and always ready to show their ugly heads. If no one has talked about the seven deadly sins in a book about copywriting before, it certainly isn't because the authors weren't aware of them. We are all very well aware of the following.

- **Gluttony** forms the basis of the billions of pounds spent each year on industries that produce things like sweets, cakes, desserts, preserves and so on, as well as the billions spent, paradoxically enough, on diet products and all kinds of methods purporting to help people lose weight.

- **Avarice** has made a fortune for banks, stockbrokers, investment consultants etc.

- **Envy** of what the neighbours own is the single, greatest motivating factor of our consumer-oriented society.

- **Pride** sells Cartier watches, flashy and expensive cars, perfumes, clothes, dream homes and thousands of other items that people don't really 'need'.

- **Laziness** is the driving force behind mail order sales, and also makes people buy all those gadgets, instant foods, handy tools etc. that are supposed to make life so much easier.

- **Lust** sells X-rated movies, videos, magazines and books, and almost anything else you can imagine. 'Pretty girls make sales' as the saying goes, and this is often quite true! Just look at the ads on TV and in magazines – they're full of pretty girls wearing less and less clothing. If they didn't sell, they wouldn't be there!

- **Anger** works best in the area of politics, and can even result in revolutions and social upheavals on a mass scale.

Are we, then, the instruments of Satan because we write sales letters? It is up to you to answer this question for yourself. The only advice I can offer is that if the product you're trying to sell is a good one and can really help people, then don't hesitate to rely on the motivating factors which deeply affect the people you're trying to reach.

We live in a material world (as the song says), in a consumer-oriented society, at the dawn of the 21st century, and even if you want to change the world, you still have to accept the rules that apply and play the cards you're dealt.

One thing is for certain, the more you know about human nature, the more enthusiastic you'll become. You'll quickly realise, as you progress in this field, that people are basically honest, sensitive, enthusiastic, kind, fairly intelligent – and idealistic!

In conclusion, keep the seven deadly sins in mind when trying to sell something, and see if there's some way you can make them work for you. You can also make use of the host of less deadly sins that all people succumb to at one time or another, but that would take another book to explain!

Now, what about you and your product?

Now take a moment to think about the product or service you're offering to people. To what motivating factors does it appeal?

Name of product or service

- My product (or service) will allow buyers to satisfy their needs for:

_____

_____

_____

- It corresponds to their desire (sin) of:

_____

_____

_____

- Are there any additional arguments you can make to help them satisfy their needs?

_____

_____

_____

Now, Stop! You already know too much to make the right kinds of promises for the target group you've chosen. And if your promise is a good one, the chances are very good that you can come up with an excellent headline which, as we've said, is the key to success in copywriting.

But if the heart of publicity is to make promises, then you still have to promise something that people want!

And there will always be something, or someone, standing in your way. We're going to find out exactly what that something or someone is in the next chapter and how to get rid of it.

SUMMARY

Experts have developed systems for decoding the human personality. These systems can become precious tools for formulating effective promises and excellent advertising headlines.

1. **Maslow's pyramid of five fundamental needs:**

   - physiological;
   - security;
   - love and belonging;
   - recognition;
   - self-realisation.

2. **The seven deadly sins:**

   - avarice;
   - anger;
   - envy;
   - gluttony;
   - lust;
   - pride;
   - laziness.

CHAPTER 4

Your greatest enemy – and how to eliminate it

As we said earlier, the best way to make your clients want to know who you are, to make them read your message, and arouse their interest in you and your offer, is to talk about them, their problems, their desires, their needs etc. Because, in fact, when you come right down to it, nothing else really interests them.

What about you?

Are you any different?

The answer is NO!

Even if you think you're concerned more about other people than yourself, even if you've taken great pains to discover other people's preoccupations, spheres of interest and so on, rest assured that you too possess a very developed ego. *Ego* means 'I' in Latin. Having a healthy ego means that you like hearing people talk about you, especially in flattering terms and that you don't mind being the centre of attention from time to time. And you also tend to think, like everyone else, that the whole world is just like you, that everyone thinks the way you do, lives the way you do and has the same problems as you do . . .

THIS IS NOT TRUE!

To become a good copywriter, you have to eliminate your greatest enemy: your own ego.

Doing this is easier said than done! This is because your ego is like a many-headed beast – the Greeks called it a 'Hydra'. You think you can get rid of it by cutting off one, two or three of its heads. But, as soon as you do that, more heads grow and take their place. . .

So what you need is a powerful and radical technique. And, in this chapter, I'm going to explain just such a technique, one that I've developed and which you can use to track down, corner and flush out all traces of your own ego . . .

The king of words in all languages – and how to make it work for you!

Advertising writers have always asked themselves what the most important word in their various languages is, i.e. which word provokes the most interest in their readers.

John Caples, one of the most famous copywriters in direct marketing, analysed 100 of the top performing advertising headlines to determine which word was used most often. Here are the results:

- the word *you* was used 31 times;
- this word *your* was used 14 times.

Then came words like *how*, *new* etc., but with much less frequency. This corresponds precisely to what Dr Flesch (author and communications expert) calls 'human self-interest': personal pronouns (first and second person), and their corresponding adjectives and possessive pronouns, refer to the people you are addressing.

The astonishing results of a study of 150 successful direct mail campaigns

Using a computer programme that I designed, I conducted a study of 150 'headlines' for direct mail campaigns that had produced exceptional responses.
Result?

- The word *you* appeared most often, with 44 instances.
- *Your* followed, with 19 instances.

Then came words like *how*, *who*, *it* etc.

And what about the texts themselves? Are they governed by different rules? Let's take a look.

I compiled the texts of eight ad writers, considered to be the best in their field, by choosing some of the best examples of their work (in terms of returns and benefits). Here's what I found: out of a total of 8,930 words there were, in decreasing order:

- 405 instances of the word *you*;

- 158 instances of the word *I*;
- 143 instances of the word *your*;

. . . followed by smaller groups like *who* (97 instances), *I'm, I'd, I'll* (92 instances) and so on.

When is the word 'I' important?

This is one of the more subtle aspects of commercial ad writing that few people understand. It is a well-guarded secret.

Professor Vogele (a German industrial psychologist specialising in direct marketing), for example, states that:

> Second person singular and plural pronouns (*you*) and their derivatives (*your, you're, yours* etc.) are 'reinforcers' while first person singular and plural pronouns (*I – we*) and their derivatives (*my, mine, our, ours* etc.) are 'filters'. Weigh the scale down on the side of reinforcers. A correct proportion would be 75 per cent *you, yours* etc. and 25 per cent *I, we* etc.

I – we and their derivatives are important when used as testimonials. And, as all direct marketing professionals know, the 'testimonial' is one of the best leverage tools in sales.

I – we (and derivatives) are important when used in the context of sincere and believable testimonials, where people express what they feel in a way that allows the reader to identify with them.

On the other hand, the *I – we* form can be used to express the equivalent of 'Look at me, see how beautiful (or handsome) I am, how intelligent, how superior I am, I . . . I . . . I . . . etc.' This is even worse than a filter – it's a total *stop*!

The secret of an extraordinary sales text

We will start by studying one of the most extraordinary texts available to us: an ad for the Aubanel Company, which first appeared in newspapers and magazines over 50 years ago, and is still used today (you'll find the text reproduced in full on pages 44–45).

Since this is a direct mail marketing ad, its effectiveness can be judged by the number of responses it produces: no responses, and the ad is abandoned. Most ads of this type don't last longer than a year. So 50 years is an all-time record!

Because the ad is written in the 'testimonial' style, the *I* pronouns predominate. Here's how our Egometer (a simple bar chart to illustrate the use of the words *I/me* and *you/your*) broke this ad down (*I*s are represented by a light grey bar, and *you*s by a dark grey bar):

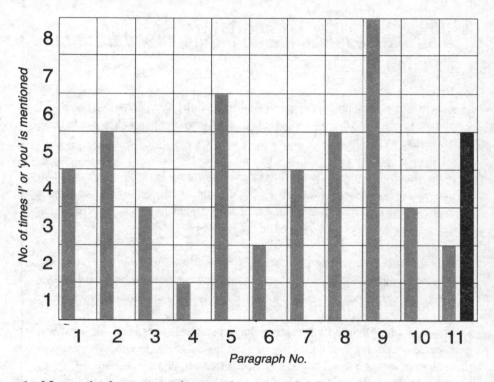

1. Not a single paragraph scored zero on the Egometer. They all have either I-testimonials or *you*s. Observe the pattern of increase and decrease. The reader's interest cannot be kept at its maximum level all the time. The aim is to create variety, and push the level of interest gradually higher and higher.

2. Note the increase in the number of *you*s at the end of the text, where the reader is encouraged to act. This is an immutable law: a good text always has more *you*s towards the end.

Just how far can you extend the limits of your memory?

A strange experience on a high speed train in Sweden . . .

1   I went into the first empty compartment I could find. I didn't know that there was already someone in there – an invisible person, whose conversation would keep me awake all night long.

2   The train pulled out of the station. I looked at the lights of Stockholm, getting dimmer in the distance. I wrapped a blanket around my shoulders and was about to stretch out on my berth and wait for sleep to come when I noticed a book, left behind by another passenger, on the opposite berth.

3   I picked it up, opened it and read the first few lines. Five minutes later, I was still reading, completely absorbed. It was like the book had been written expressly for me, by an old friend who wanted to reveal the secret of a fabulous treasure.

4   In effect, what I learned was that everyone is endowed with a fantastic memory, capable of performing unbelievably complex tasks, but that few people know how to use this amazing tool. The book explained that even the least gifted person has the ability, and cited the example of a man who, although intellectually unskilled, was able to remember the names of the 100 largest cities in the world, as well as their populations, after a single reading!

5   I found it very hard to believe that, with my tired, 40-year-old brain, I could recall all those interminable figures, dates, places and names that had made my school and college years such a nightmare, even though at that time my mind was young and fresh. I decided to find out if what this book was saying had any truth to it.

6   I pulled a timetable out of my briefcase, and started reading attentively, in the way the book prescribed. The list included 100 train stations in Sweden.

7   To my astonishment, after only one reading I was able to repeat the list in the order it was written, as well as in reverse! I could even recall exactly where each

town or city was in the list, i.e. which town was number 27, which was number 84, or 36, so deeply were the names engraved on my mind.

8 I was astounded to discover that I possessed such incredible power, and I spent the rest of the night trying more experiments, each one more difficult than the last, without feeling that I'd reached the limits of my ability.

9 Of course, I didn't just keep on doing amusing experiments. The very next day, I put my new-found faculty to work for me, and was soon able to remember everything I read, heard and saw (including musical scores, the names and faces of people I'd only met once, their addresses, telephone numbers, all my appointments etc.) with incredible accuracy. I even learned to speak a foreign language (French) in four months!

10 If I've obtained some measure of success and happiness in this life, I owe it all to this book, which revealed the secret of how my brain works.

11 I'm sure you too would like to be able to exploit this amazing mental power, which is your most precious possession, and use it to make your life a success. As an introduction to his *Complete Method*, the author, W. R. Borg, would be happy to send you a copy of *The Laws of Eternal Success*, a booklet that tells you a lot more about his discovery than I can in this short letter. The offer is available to anyone who wishes to improve his or her memory.

Here's the address:

E. Dorlier

How to set up your own 'Egometer'

You can set up your own 'Egometer': use the above Aubanel advertisement as an example. Start by underlining and counting up all indications of your own ego in red, both in the headline and in the text itself:

I

I'm

I'd

I've

Me

My

Mine

We

We'd

We've

We're

Our

Ours

Now look at the example of a mail order company letter (below) and repeat the process: underline all words connected to your ego (I-words) in red.

Dear Reader,

If only we could be talking face to face, seated in the comfortable armchairs in my office!

We'd have a coffee together (I make excellent coffee!), you could smoke a cigarette, and we'd talk about your business, and what I can do to make it grow.

What I am is an expert in sales, or to be more precise, a specialist in multiplying sales. My work consists of giving companies advice on how to develop their sales and their clientele.

What makes me qualified to do this?

First, the fact that I created and managed a business over a period of 20 years, a business which I started from scratch, and which ended up employing over 200 people.

The business I'm talking about was a mail order company!

This means that my clients, the people who bought

---

my products, only received a letter and a catalogue, and it was this letter and this catalogue, as well as a simple order form, that had to convince people to invest their hard-earned money in what I had to offer.

And I sold over a million items each year (things like costume jewellery and other gifts, at an average price of £8 per item, which translates into an average gross of more than £8 million per year!).

I did this every year for 20 years, and almost always with the same clients, who were always satisfied, and who kept on ordering year after year.

Always satisfied ... and even thrilled!

Why?

Because my business was founded on these two absolute principles:

A deal is only **ONE DEAL**.

A client is **A LOT OF DEALS**.

That's why I want you to become my client – because I know you'll be just as satisfied as all the others.

But what I'm offering you is not an item of jewellery. No, I'm going to show you how to go about finding your own clients – i.e. how to multiply your sales, and how to sell more, a lot more. The fee I'm asking will only be a fraction of what you'll earn by applying my techniques. The only condition is that you act quickly!

Get in touch with me as soon as possible. I can only accept a single client in any given field, and only a few clients in all, and those few once and for all.

Because, obviously, my clients have to be very impressed with my service for them to come back! And if they do come back, it means they're earning a lot of money.

> Why not be one of the select few to take advantage of 'Lucrative Ideas', and prove that you've got the right frame of mind and the talent to succeed.
>
> Because that too is indispensible – I only work with people who succeed.
>
> Think about it ... How much can a phone call cost? The first consultation is absolutely **FREE**. I'll be waiting to hear from you.

If readers object to hearing about your ego, they love hearing about themselves.

The second part of the analysis, therefore, consists of using another colour to underline all references to your readers' egos:

You

You'd

You've

You're

Your

Yours

Do this exercise for each letter you write. When you're finished, carefully count up all the *you* references, paragraph by paragraph. Then transfer your findings to the graph on page 49 below.

That's all there is to it. You now know how to create an 'Egometer'. Don't forget that there is a purpose to all this: writing effective headlines and sales letters. The same rules apply to both headline and text – talk about your readers, not about yourself.

You now know what motivates your readers. You know they're interested in themselves and not in you. You know how to measure the presence of your own ego in a letter. The less your ego intrudes, the better. Ideally the *you/I* ratio would be heavily in favour of the *yous*. In our second example, the ratio was very low, even though the letter was written by a professional.

Establishing the right ratio in your heading is a lot easier, since you only need to use a few words.

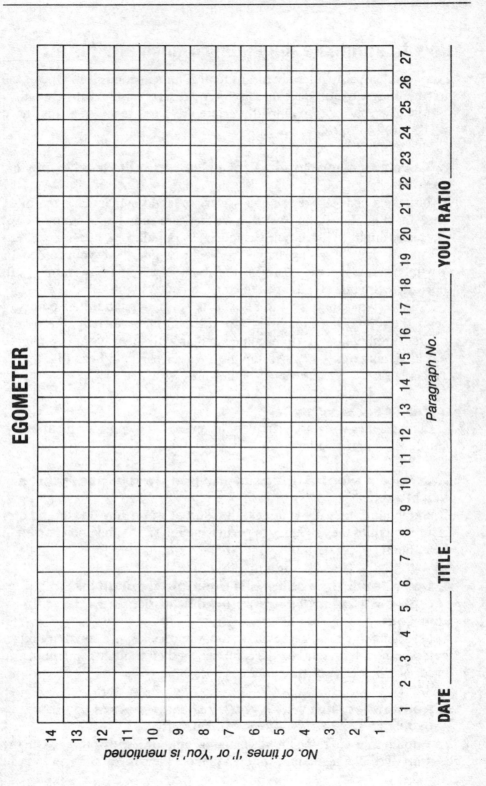

EGOMETER

No. of times 'I' or 'You' is mentioned

Paragraph No.

DATE _____ TITLE _____ YOU/I RATIO

How to eliminate the enemy – once and for all

The word 'empathy' literally means to 'feel for someone else'. One of the first qualities you must develop as a copywriter is precisely that – empathy.

How can you develop empathy? Here are a few techniques that have worked well for me.

1. Take any opportunity that arises to talk to all kinds of people

If you take a taxi, talk to the taxi driver. In fact, you should listen more than you talk. Remember, we all have two ears and only one mouth. So, you really ought to listen twice as much as you talk!

Talk to your cleaning lady, the security guard at your office or apartment building, the postman, the shopkeepers you buy from . . . in short, with anyone you happen to come in contact with.

Listen to what they have to say and try to understand their points of view, their preoccupations, their problems. Their mental universe is different from yours: try to become familiar with the way they think.

While doing this, you must stop the little voice in your head that always criticises others. Accept people as they are.

2. Vary your reading

Read magazines with large circulations, even if you consider them below your level of appreciation.

3. Create a mental image of the people to whom you're writing

Think about their daily routines, the kind of work they do, the kind of leisure activities they're likely to participate in. Try to imagine yourself in their shoes.

4. Get a few other people, if possible from different social, cultural and professional backgrounds, to read your text

Listen attentively to what they have to say and make sure you don't reject their comments outright: on the contrary, let their thoughts sink in before deciding whether to dismiss them or not.

5. Remember that when you exchange points of view with another person, you both benefit

You don't lose anything by exchanging opinions with others. On the contrary, you can maintain your own point of view if you wish or you can modify it to include what other people have to say. In addition, new ways of looking at a problem may arise during your discussions, ways that you'd never have thought of yourself.

6. During conversations, summarise what the other person has just told you and ask if your summary is accurate
This is an excellent technique for developing empathy.

7. Important! Take notes!
Whenever you come across an idea, or a frame of mind, a word or expression that is unfamiliar to you, but which your prospective clients are used to hearing, *write it down!* It's so easy to forget these little things. And they are very helpful when you're trying to come up with a good headline – recalling such phrases and ideas gets you right back into the minds of the people you're trying to reach.

Not talking about yourself does not mean forgetting who you are!

Empathy, or the ability to place yourself in the minds of your prospective clients, is one of the main qualities of a good copywriter. But it's not enough: you also have to be able to express your empathy with subtlety, in a way that reaches right to the heart of your clients and that makes them act, convincing even the most hesitant and reluctant buyers to take a chance on your product or service. How can you do this?

Just because you don't talk about yourself doesn't mean you have to forget about your personality. On the contrary, draw from your own emotional experiences, use events and personal relationships that have affected you strongly, to add impact to your text. Here are some examples.

1. Let your personality express itself
Don't be afraid to get intimate. Remember, you're writing a personal letter, not a circular.

2. Use a narrative style
In his book *Fund Raising Letters*, Jerry Huntsinger gives an example. Instead of saying, 'Poverty is a real curse for the people living in the countryside, because they can't buy the tools they need for farming. . .', you could write, 'I woke up this morning thinking about all those hungry

villagers; I'd love to be able to give them the rake and sprinkler from my own garden. . .'.

3. Share intimate feelings
Don't hesitate to talk about fears, love, suffering, generosity, worry etc. if your product or service calls for it.

4. Find an image which corresponds to each important point in your presentation

- Sound
- Sight
- Touch
- Smell
- Taste

Each image should act as a clear illustration of what you're trying to say.

5. Present your opinions in a positive way
Don't say maybe, if, eventually, possible etc. Just say clearly what you think: you have to show people that deep down inside you are convinced that your product or service is good, that you'd buy it yourself and therefore that your prospective clients should buy it as well.

SUMMARY

- You're no different from other people: you have a very strong ego. But you must be able to silence it and put yourself in other people's minds – you have to think, feel and react like them.
- By trying to see the world the way other people do, you can learn to understand them, resolve their problems, fulfil their desires and satisfy their needs.
- Get into the habit of analysing your texts with an Egometer.

CHAPTER **5**

The tricks used by professionals to make your 'headlines' work

If I were to sell you just the information contained in this single chapter, and base my price on what it could earn for you, I would have to charge you a small fortune.

The basic problem is simple: how to attract the attention of people who don't know you, who have a thousand and one preoccupations of their own – which they usually consider to be extremely important – and, most importantly, who haven't asked you for anything!

Clearly, these people do not even know you exist, so deeply concerned are they with their own thoughts; and you want to come along and get them to stop everything and listen to you, and finally do what you want them to do . . . not an easy task.

How to get an exceptional response

If you invest a few minutes of careful scrutiny now, as soon as you put down this book, the headlines you create and refine will result in exceptional responses for you.

And I mean exceptional!

This is because the difference between a mediocre headline and one that produces exceptional responses is often very subtle and discreet, depending on the choice and placement of a single word.

It's a little like the way a catalyst acts in certain chemical reactions: although present only in minute quantities, it precipitates the relatively enormous reaction sought by the chemist. On the other hand, if it is absent, you may use huge quantities of energy, machinery and materials and still not get the result you want.

How to put a catalyst in your headline

How can you learn to add a catalyst to your headline?

Keep reading on . . .

'Your first 15 words count for more than the 15,000 words that follow!'

Bob Stone, one of the best-known copywriters in the world, made that statement. And my experience in the field has always confirmed his opinion: your headline, those first few words, often chosen in haste, count for 50 per cent of the success of your entire letter. It's astounding, incredible, very hard to admit – and yet the facts speak for themselves:

50 per cent of a letter's success depends on the headline!

My experience has also often demonstrated that copywriters who are just starting out learn rapidly to appreciate the crucial importance of a good headline. All right. They quickly understand that without a good headline, a letter immediately loses 80 per cent of its effectiveness. Perfect.

On the other hand, and quite paradoxically, they all (and I mean all of them!) seem to make the same mistake:

All beginners forget to spend more than 50 per cent of their time finding an excellent headline.

And this is a mistake which often has serious consequences: the headlines they come up with are very often mediocre, not because these people are not good copywriters, but simply because they didn't take enough time to develop them.

If you're going to retain just one single message from this entire book, please make it this one: **work on your headline!** Spend 80 per cent of your time developing an excellent headline and 20 per cent on the rest of the mailing. Not the opposite!

Why 90 per cent of amateur copywriters never get their projects off the ground

When I started writing this book, I thought I'd put this sentence at the bottom of each page: **work on your headline**. I wanted to devote 80 per cent of the book to writing effective headlines and only 20 per cent to the rest. However, I changed my mind, because I thought that a lot of readers wouldn't appreciate such relentless emphasis on what seems like a simple subject. If they only knew. . .

The great copywriters of the world are under no illusions: certainly they may be able to create an excellent headline in record time, perfectly tuned to the product or service they are presenting; but they also know that they may have to create, and then discard, a host of other headlines first, slowly and painstakingly working towards the one that is just right. And, above all, these great copywriters spend an amount of time that any amateur copywriter would consider completely disproportionate. . . Just to come up with the perfect headline!

In my conferences and seminars on copywriting, I've trained hundreds of amateurs, some of whom have since become excellent professionals. But, despite my supplications, my repeated warnings and entreaties, 90 per cent of my students failed on their first attempt to create an effective headline!

The reason was always the same: they didn't spend enough time working on it.

Here, for example, are some of the headlines presented to me by these amateur copywriters:

How much do you think a robbery in your home costs you?

This sentence should have contained something 'shocking'; such as a phrase from a newspaper headline. Also, no promise is made. In addition, readers are obliged to think about a negative and very unpleasant event. Result: they only want to do one thing – forget it. All this despite the fact that the product, a new kind of alarm system for the home, lends itself very well to a 'dramatic' headline.

Interestingly enough, the entire sales letter that followed this header did not make a single promise and instead spent a lot of time describing the technical characteristics of the product (certainly very interesting to the manufacturer!), without ever citing any of the advantages or benefits consumers could expect.

Some of your clients don't pay their bills . . .

A simple statement. No promise, no benefits. . .

Do all your gourmet shopping directly and effortlessly at our deli!

An extremely weak advantage: why do your shopping at the deli at all?

Discover how to make your home environment even more beautiful

A very, very weak promise. This is a wishy-washy headline that does not attract people.

Now you, too, have the power to create . . .

No promise, with an extremely vague and weak benefit, based on an unusual motivating factor (need for self-fulfilment).

You're one of the lucky ones!

No clear benefits, not to be taken seriously, even though the product is serious enough – top of the range, made-to-measure furniture. . .

From now on, let your neighbours worry about being robbed, not you!

Too long, with the chance that people will understand exactly the opposite of what you want them to understand. Avoid a negative approach: arousing questions and negative attitudes in your readers may very well make them feel uneasy (in this case guilty about wishing harm to their neighbours) and disturb their pre-purchase attitude (here the product is designed to help the buyer, but they may prefer getting it somewhere else because of your callous attitude towards neighbours). The first time I read it, I understood that 'I want my neighbours to get robbed'!

No promises are made, no advantages are stated.

Let Jon G. and Louise M. prepare your astral horoscope without the use of a computer...

No promise, practically no advantages and even a negative approach (these days computers help astrologers make almost infinite numbers of calculations with ease, and prepare very accurate charts, which can then be interpreted by experts . . .). Referring to the names of unknown persons accomplishes absolutely nothing (except to flatter the egos of the persons involved).

To all heads of business: if you want to remain anonymous, then don't read this letter.

Once again, avoid the negative approach: this headline makes readers want to do only one thing – throw the letter in the bin! Never use a full stop at the end of a headline – a full stop is like a stop sign on the road, while a good headline should read like a huge green light! No promise is made (there is an underlying promise, but it must be guessed) and no explicit benefits are stated.

Note that the student used this headline as a sub-heading, the heading itself being the logo of the company, including address and phone number. This is a classic error which many amateur copywriters unfortunately make. They consider their product, their logo, their company, even their own name to be so important that they're just dying to put it right up at the top of the page! They do this despite the fact that it is very rare for a company name or logo to include an implicit promise or advantage for prospective clients.

Moral of the story? If you are susceptible to this kind of ego-waving, add a line to your 'Egometer' analysis which covers your name, logo etc. as if they were simple I's. . .

Also, don't commit the opposite, but just as serious, error of thinking that you can substitute your client's name, company or logo for a headline. That's not what a headline is about!

Always keep the single and unique definition of a headline in mind:

- a sentence/phrase;
- placed at the head of the text;
- which makes a promise and arouses curiosity.

To resolve your recurring problems. Finally, a solution: DBI

What is the promise? If there is one, it isn't clear. In any case, I don't have recurring problems and I'm in a hurry. Throw it in the wastebasket!

Actually, the product was a computer programme for daily planning, designed for small businesses in the region. Once again, the name of the company, DBI, was used in the headline. Not only does it accomplish nothing, it complicates matters because people don't know what the letters stand for!

Result? The student informed us that the client was in a hurry and sent out an initial mailing of 1,000 letters. The responses were devastating: one reply, non-committal; leading to zero orders!

And yet, the product was an excellent one. When it was later reintroduced on to the market, once again through direct mail, but with a much more rigorous approach to the copywriting, and with a headline that had been well thought out, and which was the fruit of long labour, it did very well.

Remember that your headline should really be one true sentence: if yours can be broken down into two parts, like this one, then work on it some more, until you end up with one single, short, logical, fluid and simple headline!

I've been saving the best (actually the worst) for last: many of the letters I received had no headline at all!!

It sounds absolutely incredible, until you've experienced it yourself: I always insist on the importance of using an effective headline throughout my seminars and conferences, even to the point of boring my listeners . . .

And still, every time without fail, at least 20 per cent of my student copywriters go ahead and submit sales letters with no headline whatsoever!

So I'm going to repeat it one more time: 50 per cent of a sales letter's success depends solely on the headline. All tests conducted on the subject have always and conclusively shown that this is true. Therefore, if you deprive your text of an effective headline, you must automatically expect to get only very mediocre responses.

Now let's take a look at the most effective techniques for developing good headlines.

How to distract your prospects from their usual preoccupations!

There are four ways in which you can break through the barrier of your client's own worries, thoughts and other preoccupations.

1. Promise an advantage or benefit, the satisfaction of one of their desires or needs, and whenever possible the strongest or most urgent one you can think of. (And we've just given you a detailed explanation of how to find that urgent need or desire in Chapter 4.)

2. Make a promise (this is actually the same thing, presented in a different way) to help avoid an inconvenience, pain, a lack of something or a problem.

3. Arouse curiosity (one of humanity's basic motivating forces).

4. Announce some important news (which is another way of arousing curiosity).

Say, for example, that you're selling a remedy for insomnia, you could try to hook your clients by emphasising:

sleep, or

how to conquer insomnia.

Most often, the positive approach (*sleep*) will produce the best results. But, sometimes, the negative approach works better, as for example with corns on the feet, shyness, rheumatism and other somewhat embarrassing disorders.

The techniques of arousing curiosity and breaking some important news always work well, and can easily be made to accompany a promise.

New! Now here's a way to get rid of fatigue once and for all!

Readers know right off that this is news – i.e. something new. They ask themselves how they can stop being tired (curiosity) and are given a promise (to get rid of fatigue). Another way of stating it might be:

At last! A way to stay in top shape – and overflow with energy.

What the professionals do to make their headlines succeed

Every professional copywriter has his or her own personal formula. When you acquire some experience, you'll be able to recognise different styles:

you'll be able to say, 'This sales letter must have been written by the X agency. . . '. A copywriter's formula is often a synthesis of all the other formulas they learned from other professionals, as well as their own experience in the field.

So, first use the most successful and proven formulae you can find, and verify their effectiveness yourself.

The *Reader's Digest* formula

David Ogilvy, John Caples and other advertising greats often refer to *Reader's Digest* and its approach. In fact, the *Reader's Digest* approach is based on a number of formulae. Here are some of their most frequently used headlines.

- How to . . .
- Seven steps to . . .
- Ten ways to . . .
- A New Scientific Discovery . . .
- The secret of . . .
- Why . . .?
- What happens when . . .?
- Should you . . .?
- Are you . . .?
- How can you . . .?
- An absolutely sure-fire way to . . .
- Your guide to . . .

Use one formula. Adapt it to suit the personality of your product, your business etc. Adjust it and refine it as much as you wish, but stick to one formula at a time.

If we go on to study some of the *Reader's Digest* campaigns, we find the following topics crop up frequently.

Health

Health is a subject that recurs very frequently. Here are some examples:

- Stop smoking

- Three little secrets to stay in great shape

- Sexual impotence – what you should know about it

- How to fight stress

- Protecting yourself against the common cold

- Seven steps for getting thin
- Can you choose your child's sex?
- Finally – an anti-cancer diet
- Victory over virus

Self-improvement

- Seven keys for thinking better
- Get rid of your double chin
- Awaken the child sleeping inside you
- Say it in a letter
- How to improve your voice
- The winning secret
- Nourish your brain

Children

- How to succeed without a university degree
- What have you got out of your studies?
- Pros and cons of special schools
- Are you sure you know your children?
- When little kids become little brats
- Education through the eyes of an adolescent

Couples

- Love for ever
- Spouses and lovers
- Revelations on male sexuality
- What makes a man sexy?
- Twenty proposals on love
- Should you tell the person you love everything?

- What makes a woman attractive?
- Why don't men talk to their wives?

Jobs

- Strategies for finding a job
- Why bosses work like slaves
- Whatever happened to your pay rise?
- Living with computers
- Seven steps to finding a job
- How to become a leader
- Career: get a fast start and go farther

Money

- Learn how to write your will
- How to get your money back
- The car insurance labyrinth
- Reduce your income taxes

Reader's Digest has a monthly circulation of 28,000,000 copies, in 15 different languages around the globe. This kind of success is the mark of professionalism, and one which you should aspire to emulate.

Each campaign is tested and tried out in different countries; each successful campaign is noted and used as a model for other campaigns.

But *Reader's Digest* isn't the only organisation using formulae.

The favourite technique of the professionals

The technique most often used by professionals is very easy to set up: all you need is the place, the organisation (to correctly file all your clients) and knowledge of a professional 'trick'. . .

Yes, you too can pick out the best headlines in the mailings, newspapers and magazines you receive, because determining whether a headline is effective or not is very simple:

If the headline appears a number of times, over a period of days, weeks, even years, then you can safely assume that it is effective.

Why? It is very simple. . .

In direct marketing, whether in the form of a mailing or an ad in a newspaper or magazine, the judgement is immediate. In the 15 days following distribution of the mailing, 45 per cent of the total responses will be received: at the end of a month, about 80 per cent of the campaign's total responses will have been received.

Therefore, if an ad appears a number of times, or if the same headline is used for a number of large-scale mailings, then you can be sure that the headline in question is profitable and thus effective.

And I cannot over-emphasise the importance of opening a file, as soon as possible, so that you can collect all the quality mailings you receive.

Sort them by theme or by product, and do a short analysis for each one, underlining the important points and ideas which you can later use as inspiration for your own texts. When the time comes, you'll have a precious tool at your disposal, not only for designing your mailing, but also, and above all, for finding the most effective headline for your product or service.

Although the best training to become a specialist in writing good headlines is still to practise coming up with the right headline for real products, professionals do have another way of training themselves – a negative approach, if you will – which consists of endlessly criticising other writers' success.

Make no mistake about it, their criticism is constructive. All they're trying to do is discover the mechanism which made a particular headline so successful. In other words, they want to understand why it worked so well. It may look like they are spending hours and hours theorising and making propositions, when in actual fact what they're doing is refining their own talent and ability to write effective headlines.

The secret of bestselling books

Here's an unexpected way to train yourself to write headlines: study the titles of bestselling books. Editors who choose the titles for books have to deal with the same problems as copywriters. They must attract their prospective buyer's attention immediately and they must make a promise. Great titles are therefore exactly like effective headlines . . .

The moral of the story? Pay attention to the titles of books that sell well and look for the key to their success in their titles.

The best headlines in the world!

You should also know about certain headlines that have been consistently successful for 30 years or more. You can find examples in hundreds of variations, applied to different sectors and widely differing products, which have usually also been successful, and **nothing attracts success like success.**

Of course, we're not suggesting you copy a successful headline word for word, but neither do you have to go out and reinvent the wheel every time you want to write a sales text. By basing your approach on proven formulae, you will save time and reduce your risks considerably.

And if, after reworking and adapting one, or a number of proven formulae, you achieve success of your own, you will have earned it!

So, where can you find these proven formulae?

Here is a selection of some of the best headlines in the world, which we've put together from the best sources we could find.

Don't forget that each one is the result of over 50 years' experience and has had millions of pounds invested in it.

- They all laughed when I sat down at the piano, but when I started playing. . !
- *A little mistake which cost this farmer £20,000 a year. . .*
- Can you pick out the ten decorating mistakes in this picture?
- *So often a bridesmaid, but never a bride. . .*
- Advice to women whose husbands never seem to be able to save money – from a married woman
- *Why certain foods 'explode' in your stomach*
- Is the life of a child worth £5 to you?
- *How I went from failure to success in sales*
- How to do your Christmas shopping in five minutes
- *How I started a new life with £25*
- How to be proud of your cooking
- *To people who want to write – but who can't get started . . .*
- To women who look older than their age . . .
- *53 reasons why you should have answered this ad last week*

- I didn't have time to go to the university, so I studied at home by reading. . .
- *Play the guitar in seven days or your money back!*
- Seven ways to conquer the habit of over-eating
- *To all men who want to stop working one day*
- A warning to anyone who wants to be financially independent in five years
- *When doctors don't feel well, here's what they do*
- Get rid of your money problems once and for all
- *How I improved my memory in one night*
- How I made a fortune with a crazy idea
- *How to make friends and influence people*
- Men who 'know it all' can skip this page
- *The best way to get rich – if you're lazy*
- Even deaf people can hear the whispers
- *The secret reason people like you*
- Who else wants to look like a movie star?
- *Free for wives – £20 for everyone else*
- Get twice your money back if this isn't the best onion soup you've ever tasted!
- *Which of these five skin problems would you like to cure?*
- To men who are 35 or older and who still aren't satisfied
- *How a strange accident saved me from going bald*
- Don't buy a computer until you've seen the one that caused a sensation at the last International Computer Convention
- *Pay less for car insurance if you're a careful driver*
- 'Here, Carol, an extra £2,300. Am I making good money now or not?'
- *What makes a woman desirable?*

And here are two very interesting tricks of the trade.

- Out of the best 101 headlines in the United States, 23 start with the word 'how' which seems to be a veritable key to success, according to specialists in the field. Think about it!

- The imperative form (Don't do this . . . or Do that . . . Get rid of this . . . etc.) is often used because it incites readers to act, to move and so on. This provocation (if put to good use, especially in sales letters) is a very precious tool.

OK, you now know about the importance of an effective headline and about all the errors to avoid when working on your first attempts to write a good one. We've looked at the best professional formulae for building effective headlines and we've reviewed some of the best headlines in the world. Now it's time to put all this theory into practice!

Copywriters who are starting out have the same problem as novelists who want to start a new book: a haunting fear of the blank page in front of them. . .

How to create a successful headline with ease

So, how can you automatically create excellent headlines? Is there a sure and tested way to come up with dozens of effective headlines with ease?

Yes, there is, and we're going to take a look at it now. It may not have been invented by a genius, but it works, and it works well.

Some writers have their little ticks and tricks, their phobias and manias, their special little habits (for example, a writer I know spends his morning sharpening all his pencils, drinking five or six cups of strong coffee and reading three newspapers from cover to cover). These habits are usually excuses to procrastinate – to put off getting down to some real work for as long as possible.

On the other hand, I know an author whose books are practically always bestsellers, who has these simple but infallible tricks for getting started.

1. Every time he has to do some work, he sets a limit on the amount of time he has to spend at his desk (usually between ten minutes and an hour). If he puts in the time required, he gives himself a reward.

2. As soon as he sits down at his desk, he takes a sheet of paper and, practically without thinking about it, starts writing the continuation of wherever he left off last time. Important: note that he keeps writing, whatever the quality happens to be. The important thing is to keep the

pen moving across the paper (or to keep punching the keys on the computer).

And, like working in the clutch on a new car, the quality comes soon enough, as his faculties get sharper, so that in a very short time he's working at top capacity. He then looks over the first couple of paragraphs and corrects them, or even throws them away and starts again.

As I said, this 'trick' for getting started is simple, easy and infallible. Try it and you'll quickly see how well it works.

Indeed, there's no secret way to write great headlines. You have to work on them and continually practise finding the one that's best.

For beginners, a headline may be nothing more than a few well-chosen words. For professionals, a great headline is more like a masterpiece: creating it takes years of study, practice, mistakes, improving and refining the techniques of their writing, developing their art to its highest degree . . .

If you become an artist, an expert at creating great headlines, then you will automatically be an excellent copywriter.

A springboard for creating more successful headlines

Here's a final technique for coming up with great headlines. I got it from one of the truly great professional copywriters, who told me he considered it the 'crux of his creativity' – without it, he'd collapse. . .

Here it is. It's based on the mental process associated with creativity, which we'll be looking at later on in this book. Our brain is like a machine, designed to produce answers. The only problem lies in asking the right questions! In other words, 'A well-phrased question is half the answer!' And this is especially true for headlines.

On the following pages, you'll find a guide for finding the factors which can motivate your readers to buy. You'll also find the beginnings of a few headlines which you then have to complete. The question you will be asked is: 'How should the following sentence be completed?'

Fill out at least two 'creation forms', as set out below, for each product you have, writing down anything that comes to mind. Don't criticise yourself. You'll select the best of your headlines later on.

Here is some advice on using this technique.

1. If a suggested formula doesn't inspire you – just skip it.

2. Give yourself a fair amount of time to really consider what the motivating factors of your target clients are.

3. Wait at least a day between writing all your potential headlines, and going back and selecting the best ones (in other words, sleep on it).

4. Paste the best headlines on squares of cardboard and show them to people you know, asking which ones they find most effective.

Creation Form

Product: _____

- What will this product/service do for me? _____

_____

- How will it help me satisfy my physiological needs? _____

_____

- How will it help me satisfy my need for security? _____

_____

- How will it help me satisfy my need for love and belonging? _____

_____

- How will it help me satisfy my need for recognition? _____

_____

- How will it help satisfy my need for self-fulfilment? _____

_____

- What does this have to do with my gluttony? _____

_____

- With my greed? _____

- With my pride? _____

- With my laziness? _____

- With my desire and lust? _____

- With my anger? _____

- How will this help me fight loneliness? _____

- How can it help me protect my rights? _____

- How will it help me conquer my fears? _____

- How will it help me to assert myself, become a stronger person? ____
_____

- How will it help me overcome my feelings of guilt? _____
_____

- How will it give me more confidence and help me overcome my
inner conviction of not living up to my full potential? _____
_____

- In short, what am I going to be able to save – earn – accomplish by
using this product or service? _____
_____

- How can it help me eliminate or reduce risks, worries, losses,
mistakes and all kinds of other negative factors? _____
_____

- What is it that will make me so curious I'll just have to read your
text? Make me curious enough to want to know more! _____
_____

- How . . . _____

- How I became . . . _____

- How I have . . . _____

- Why . . . _____

- What . . . _____

- Who else . . . _____

- Which . . . _____

- What is it . . . _____

- In which way . . . _____

- When . . . _____

- Where . . . _____
- How much . . . _____
- Yes, you too . . . _____
- You . . . _____
- Free: _____
- New: _____
- Here . . . _____
- Now . . . _____
- Finally . . . _____
- The secret . . . _____
- Warning to . . . _____
- We are looking for . . . _____
- Have you ever . . . _____
- Do you . . . _____
- Have you ever seen . . . _____
- Is your . . . _____
- Discover . . . _____
- Get . . . _____
- Get rid of . . . _____
- You should know that . . . _____
- Accept . . . _____
- Dare . . . _____
- Learn . . . _____
- Regain . . . _____
- Master . . . _____
- Have . . . _____

- Be . . . _____
- Make money . . . _____
- Change . . . _____
- Become . . . _____
- Ask . . . _____
- Use . . . _____
- Listen . . . _____
- Do . . . _____
- Own . . . _____
- Participate . . . _____
- Improve . . . _____
- Reveal . . . _____
- Let yourself . . . _____
- Choose . . . _____
- Try . . . _____
- Win/earn . . . _____
- Save . . . _____
- Live . . . _____
- Take . . . _____
- Don't let . . . _____
- Imagine . . . _____
- Seven steps for . . . _____
- Ten ways to . . . _____
- Your guide to . . . _____
- The latest about/on . . . _____

SUMMARY

- Fifty per cent of a sales letter's success depends entirely on its headline. You should therefore set aside 50 per cent of your time for developing the best possible headline.
- Experience has shown that amateur copywriters usually spend a lot less time than that on their headlines and that is the main reason they don't achieve the success they expect. Make sure you don't make the same mistake. Force yourself to spend the necessary time working on your headlines, develop an efficient and professional attitude, and practise regularly.
- Use tested formulae to write successful headlines: you'll waste less time and be more effective.
- Get into the habit of using a creation form to collect and then select your best headlines.

CHAPTER 6

An infallible way to select your best headline

Why are some headlines so successful, while others seem to fall flat?

The best way to answer this question is to analyse some excellent headlines. Look at this one, for example:

Which of these languages would you like to speak?

This excellent headline includes a promise (speaking a foreign language) and a question. It appeals to thè following motivating factors:

- curiosity;
- self-fulfilment;
- pride.

How I got rid of my money problems.

The 'how' promises a solution. A lot of people have to deal with money problems. 'Got rid of' suggests action, which is also a kind of promise. This headline was used to sell a book on starting your own lucrative business at home. It added 15 per cent in supplementary sales when compared with the headline 'How to start your own small and profitable business in the comfort of your own home'.

   The motivations here are:

- curiosity;
- security;
- envy;
- gain.

Who else wants a free copy of our little book on hypnosis?

This headline contains one of the magic words: free. Saying 'who else' implies that other people have already taken advantage of the offer, and arouses the new reader's natural tendency to envy, or even to be jealous of what other people have.

The motivations here are:

- belonging;
- envy;
- self-fulfilment;
- self-affirmation.

To all of you out there who are suffering. . .

Readers who are suffering stop there because they are personally concerned. The trick lies in the fact that a lot of people suffer from one kind of disorder or another, and that suffering (actually getting rid of suffering) is a very basic motivating factor.

The motivations here are:

- physiological;
- belonging.

The amazing potential of memory

The key word here is 'amazing'. It arouses curiosity. The word 'memory' qualifies readers, i.e. it eliminates anyone who isn't interested in the subject of memory. The word potential implies a promise.

The motivations are:

- curiosity;
- self-fulfilment.

How I stopped smoking for good

Here again we find the magic word 'how'; the word 'smoking' qualifies the kind of reader interested and the phrase 'for good' strengthens the promise made in 'how I stopped'.

The motivations are:

- curiosity;
- avoiding negative things;
- guilt;
- envy.

Bachelors: *change the way you date*

The word 'bachelors' qualifies the clientele; 'change the way you date' is an implicit promise – the rest of the text will explain how to go about accomplishing this.

One of the advantages of this headline is that it's very short and therefore dynamic. A disadvantage is that the promise is not very explicit. Fortunately, it was accompanied by a visual (a picture of a smiling man and woman).

As John Caples comments: 'The best headlines are composed of ideas that sell, expressed in the simplest possible way.'

The motivations here are:

■ a need for love and belonging;
■ a desire for pleasure.

Do not buy any. . .

Everybody's telling people to buy more! This approach is intriguing because it runs counter to our expectations.

What do you think the motivations are here?

Cheaper car insurance – if you're a careful driver

'Car insurance' qualifies interested readers; 'cheaper' makes a promise; if you are 'careful' it makes the promise credible.

What do you think the motivations are here?

'Here's an extra £xx . . . now do you think I make a good living?'

The word 'now' implies that some change has taken place and arouses curiosity; the extra '£xx' fulfils the need for giving pleasure, for succeeding, for being admired; 'make a good living' responds to the need for security in the form of money and remains very credible.

What are the motivations?

How I improved my memory in a single night

The promise comes through loud and clear ('improve your memory') and the phrase 'in a single night' adds an element of surprise which arouses readers' curiosity (so that they continue reading) and also reinforces the original promise.

Play the guitar in seven days or get your money back

'Play the guitar' qualifies interested readers; 'in seven days' reinforces the promise; 'your money back' makes the promise credible.

A warning to anyone who wants to achieve financial independence in the next five years

The phrase 'to anyone who' qualifies your readers; 'a warning' makes readers want to find out more and implies a promise (to avoid a problem).

Phrases like 'Careful!' or 'Your attention please!' are usually followed by some 'important advice' – something that should be read in case it does really happen to be important. Using this approach in a headline lets you take advantage of people's powerful reading habits.

What makes a woman desirable?

A bone of contention among copywriters is whether or not a headline can be phrased in the form of a question.

The answer, as far as we are concerned, is yes!

You'll find a lot of excellent headlines that pose questions. But – and there is a big but – the question must imply a promise. That is the case here. Readers expect to discover what makes women desirable.

What can we learn from these headlines?

As you can see, we have proposed a few basic ideas on how to write good headlines. Here they are in summary.

1. Qualify your readers (not too much – you want to reach the greatest number of people possible) sufficiently so that they feel they have a personal interest in finding out more about your product or service.

2. Make a promise (see Chapter 5).

3. Reinforce the promise (with words like fast, for good, once and for all etc.)

4. Arouse your readers' curiosity.

5. Make your promise credible (by offering a guarantee, a reason, a qualifying statement, for example 'If you're a careful driver. . .').

A professional technique: 'internal promotion'

If you do a good job writing your sales letter, you'll find a number of phrases or sentences that can easily be transformed into excellent headlines. This is what is meant by the term 'internal promotion'.

Read the letter set out below and try to pick out sentences that could be used as headlines. Underline them. Next, select three or four from those you've underlined. Which in your opinion seems to be the best?

Two very important people are waiting to meet you. They want to talk to you ... about yourself.

One's name is W. Clement Stone. Starting from scratch, he now controls one of the largest fortunes in the world.

The other is the celebrated Napoleon Hill. His book on personal development *Think and Grow Rich* has sold over 14 million copies.

Both these men possess the secret of transforming ideas into reality. They know:

- How to awaken the potential for success that is lying dormant inside you.

- How you can get other people to act according to your desires.

- How to help you fight fatigue and multiply your energy.

- All the recipes and all the tricks to transform the world around you by changing your mental attitude.

Because that's where the secret lies: change your way of thinking and your health will improve. Change your way of seeing and the doors of opportunity will open wide for you. Change your state of mind and others will flock to you like moths attracted to light.

W. Clement Stone and Napoleon Hill have pooled all their knowledge and all their experience into a

---

single volume. This book is a masterpiece! Two
pounds of paper and ink that are simply dynamite:

Success Through Positive Thinking

305 fascinating pages which reveal the real you to
yourself. 120,000 word-tools, 120,000 word-images
that will have a profound effect on you.

When you put this book down, you'll never be the
same again.

You'll know exactly where you are vulnerable. You'll
know what to do to succeed, and how to lead a
fuller, richer and more satisfying life.

Our answers

'Transform the world around you by changing your mental attitude'
provided the best results, followed by, 'Learn the secret of transforming
ideas into reality' and a distant third was, 'After reading this book, you'll
never be the same again'.

The 'internal promotion' technique is supported by one of the two
schools of writing headlines and headings. One school insists the headline
should be written before the rest of the text, while the other school says it's
better to write the text first. The first approach usually produces more
brilliant ideas, while the second is more reliable. Try both and see which
works best for you!

How to double the impact of your headline

This last technique is not concerned with sales letters as such (at least those
which try to use a personalised approach), but with brochures, so-called
'lift letters', flyers, booklets etc., in short any document that accompanies
the sales letter and which is likely to include illustrations.

'A picture is worth a thousand words. . .' says the proverb. All the
professionals I know have experienced this fact for themselves, especially
when working on newspaper and magazine ads, where space is so expensive. A visual can spark a product's sales, even where the headline and text
are already good.

The combination of an effective visual + headline + text results in explosive selling power.

Why? Because no matter how good a headline is, an ad without a visual has a lot more trouble attracting attention than an ad which has a visual.

How to create visuals that pay off

Here are some rules on creating visuals, culled from years of experience.

1. Photographs work better than drawings.

2. One large photograph is more effective than a number of smaller ones.

3. A photograph that suggests some action or movement is preferable to one that has no movement in it at all.

4. In decreasing order, here are the kinds of pictures that consistently show the highest returns:
- pictures of children;
- portraits;
- groups of people;
- animals;
- landscapes.

5. Show your product in action (clients will be more attracted to a picture of a pile of clean, folded laundry than to a box of detergent).

6. Always place the headline under the visual.

7. Always add a caption to the picture: as soon as your prospective client's attention is caught by the visual, he or she will read the caption (if there is one) with growing curiosity . . .

Why you have to test your headlines

Creating your headlines, improving them, giving them maximum impact, finding the right headline and the right visual – all that isn't enough. You still have to learn how to select your best headline.

It's very easy to miss out on a golden opportunity by a couple of minutes. In copywriting, all it takes is a single word!

Think about this story. An estate agent had to recruit some salespeople and placed an ad in the local newspaper. He mentioned a fairly high commission potential, around £30,000 per year. No one responded to the ad. So he lowered the commission figure to £15,000 and received a flood of applications. He then chose the best of the candidates and they all ended up earning over £30,000 a year.

In this particular instance, the estate agent was lucky – he hit on a figure than won the jackpot.

But how many copywriters are satisfied with only one per cent responses, or even less, while in fact, forgetting about the 99 per cent of cases where their approach failed?

Technique for selecting the best of your headlines

It's not enough to write a lot of headlines and make them as good as possible. You still have to determine which one is the best.

Doing a mailing is like sending out sales reps to meet your clients personally. So, who are you going to choose to represent you?

The best, of course.

You can certainly rely, to some extent, on your instinct and intelligence to select what you think are your top ten headlines. But the final decision as to which is the best must always be based on tests which are as reliable as possible and as extensive as you can afford.

If you don't have any money, you'll have to rely on the opinions of the people around you and, if possible, on the advice of any professionals you can get in touch with (they should be at least partially familiar with your target clientele).

On the other hand, if you can make even a minimum investment in some kind of market study testing, then you should do so. This will enable you to:

- select your best headline (the larger your sample clientele is, the more confident you can be of the accuracy of the results);

- calculate (we'll tell you how later on) the total amount of sales you can statistically hope to achieve by sending the same message to the rest of the target group.

Between these two extremes (an investment of between zero pounds and a few thousand, or even a few hundred thousand pounds), you should be able to locate your optimum level, taking into account the reduction of risks and costs, and the increase in profits, as opposed to the amount you invest.

How to test a headline

Market studies that test headlines are a luxury that only large or mid-size companies can afford. But you can conduct a test yourself, by using the tables below. The results should be within a one per cent margin of accuracy, if your sample group is composed of 2,000 addresses or more.

Sending 2,000 letters represents an investment of close to £380, at current postal rates. This figure should be multiplied by the number of headlines you wish to test.

The principle of testing a headline is the same as that of a horse race. You give every one the same opportunity – i.e. the same price, the same letter, the same supporting documents – everything must be identical except the headline! Then . . . may the best headline win!

Even if you're promoting a product for a company that is just starting out, or if you're starting out yourself, you can still test your headlines.

Take a good look at the table below. You'll see that if you're looking for very significant differences, then you can use a relatively small sample group.

If the size of the sample group is:	And if the percentage of sales for this sample group is:	Then the chances are 95 out of 100 that the percentage of sales for the rest of the target group will be between:
100	1	0 and 2.99
100	2	0 and 4.80
100	3	0 and 6.41
100	4	0.08 and 7.92
100	5	0.64 and 9.36
100	10	4.00 and 16.00
100	20	12.00 and 28.00
250	1	0 and 2.26
250	2	0.23 and 3.77
250	3	0.84 and 5.16
250	4	1.52 and 6.48
250	5	2.24 and 7.76
250	10	6.20 and 13.80
250	20	14.94 and 25.00
500	1	0.11 and 1.89
500	2	0.75 and 3.25
500	3	1.48 and 4.52
500	4	2.25 amd 5.75
500	5	3.05 and 6.95
500	10	7.32 and 12.68

If the size of the sample group is:	And if the percentage of sales for this sample group is:	Then the chances are 95 out of 100 that the percentage of sales for the rest of the target group will be between:
500	20	16.42 and 23.58
1,000	1	0.37 and 1.63
1,000	2	1.12 and 2.88
1,000	3	1.92 and 4.08
1,000	4	2.76 and 5.24
1,000	5	3.62 and 6.38
1,000	10	8.10 and 11.90
1,000	20	17.48 and 22.52
2,000	1	0.55 and 1.45
2,000	2	1.37 and 2.63
2,000	3	2.24 and 3.76
2,000	4	3.12 and 4.88
2,000	5	4.03 and 5.97
2,000	10	8.66 and 11.34
2,000	20	18.21 and 21.79
5,000	1	0.72 and 1.28
5,000	2	1.60 and 2.40
5,000	3	2.52 and 3.48
5,000	4	3.45 and 4.55
5,000	5	4.38 and 5.62
5,000	10	9.15 and 10.85
5,000	20	18.87 and 21.13
10,000	1	0.80 and 1.20
10,000	2	1.72 and 2.28
10,000	3	2.66 and 3.34
10,000	4	3.61 and 4.39
10,000	5	4.56 and 5.44
10,000	10	9.40 and 10.60
10,000	20	19.20 and 20.80
100,000	1	0.94 and 1.06
100,000	2	1.91 and 2.09
100,000	3	2.89 and 3.11
100,000	4	3.88 and 4.12
100,000	5	4.86 and 5.14
100,000	10	9.81 and 10.19
100,000	20	19.75 and 20.25

Here is an example in which you test the following headlines:

1. Detect people's most secret thoughts

2. Discover the benefits of 'biofeedback' free of charge, in your own home

3. How to achieve perfect mastery of yourself

4. Communicate with plants and have fun with your lie detector!

5. Do your own fascinating experiments in parapsychology!

When each of these headlines was sent to only 100 addresses the results were as follows:

1 = 0 orders
2 = 9 orders
3 = 10 orders
4 = 2 orders
5 = 3 orders

We can now eliminate headlines 1, 4, and 5, and concentrate on 2 and 3. Let's start with number 3.

If you examine the table, you'll see that with a sample mailing of only 100 addresses, you need at least 10 responses to be certain of an overall response of between 4 and 16 per cent.

This kind of test is therefore impossible to carry out on such a small sample group, unless your sales letter is very good and produces, at least in conjunction with one of the headlines, a minimum of ten responses.

Next you have to take the profit margin into account. If you have 50 per cent fewer responses, and are still able to turn a profit, then you might want to send the same message to the same group again, this time with a different headline (in this case number 2).

This strategy usually results in a little more than 50 per cent take up the second time around.

Here's another example.

You sent out 5,000 letters and receive 380 orders. If you'd only received 190 orders (i.e. 50 per cent), but still showed a profit (after deducting all your costs including mailing, product, shipping etc.), then do a second mailing. You'll get orders from people who hesitated the first time around or who were too busy to pay attention, who forgot etc. This should bring you another 160 orders. And if you use a different headline (as we suggested earlier), your second mailing could result in as many as 170 or 180 orders.

Of course, ideally you'd be testing much larger sample groups. You can then be sure of the results.

What percentage of responses signifies an effective letter?

It's impossible to answer that question. It depends on the price of your product, the quality of the mailing list etc. We can tell you that it's rare to go above 25 per cent, and that if your responses are less than 0.8 per cent you'd better write another letter. I always try to achieve at least 10 per cent (and if possible a little better) with any mailing list.

Other ways to select your best headline

There are a number of ways to test your headlines against each other and select the best one. Here are four methods which provide excellent results.

1. The 'split-run'

Certain magazines will agree to run half an issue with one of your ads and the other half with another. You keep the same text, the same visuals, and change only the headline and the code on the order form (so that you can tell which orders came from which headlines). This technique is called a 'split-run'.

If you want to test more than two headlines, choose one as your constant and test it in different magazines against the other headlines.

For example, say you want to test these three headlines:

- How to protect and sell your ideas
- How to make money with your ideas
- I'm looking for people who want to make money

You'd use 'How to make money with your ideas' as your constant; you do a split-run test in a magazine, against 'How to protect and sell your ideas'.

In another, similar magazine, you do another split-run test, this time against the headline 'I'm looking for people who want to make money'.

Result: 'How to protect. . .' yielded a lower response than 'How to make money. . .' while 'I'm looking for people. . .' yielded a better response than 'How to make money. . .'. You would therefore stick with 'I'm looking for people who want to make money' as your best headline.

If you have a new headline you want to test, you'd use 'I'm looking for people who. . .' as your constant (in other words, always use your top performing headline as your constant).

2. The telescope test

It's possible to test a number of headlines in the same print medium (magazine, newspaper, bulletin, newsletter etc.) all at the same time. To do this, the circulation must be large. You print up an insert (a leaflet inserted in a magazine) advertising your product, using your various headlines in equal numbers. For a fee, the magazine or newspaper will include the insert in one of its issues. You select the best headline based on the results of this single, 'telescopic' test.

3. Classified ads

In the classified ads section of a magazine or newspaper, run the same text twice, changing only the headline. You'll need some way of identifying which headline produced which orders – a simple way of doing this would be to add a letter to your address, for example:

1. Write today to Godefroy Publications, Post Office Box 94, London.

2. Write today to Godefroy Publications, Post Office Box 94A, London.

4. The list

You can offer a list of free booklets or articles, and use the most selected title as your eventual headline.
　Here's an example:

　Free! As part of our market information campaign, we're offering the following booklets absolutely free of charge:

- How I got rid of my money problems
- How to run a lucrative small business in your own home
- How to earn more money in your spare time
- My 35 secrets for making a fortune

　Tick the booklet you want (only one book per order please!) and return the coupon to:

SUMMARY

- Consider using an illustration to double the impact of your headline. If possible, make it:
  - a photograph
  - picturing some kind of action,
  - showing your product in action,
  - with your headline directly below it.

- To find new headlines, use the 'internal promotion' method.

- Testing your headlines is the fastest way to success.

- There are four methods available:
  - split-run;
  - telescope test;
  - classified ads;
  - free offer list.

CHAPTER 7

Offers and postscripts: how to get higher sales from your very first letter!

A 'trick' used by direct mail agencies

Direct mail agencies all suffer from one important defect: the fees they charge (and, because of the fierce competition, those fees are often stretched to the limit) prevent them from spending a lot of time on creating headlines and usually even on writing copy.

Result: they rarely produce excellent copy. Their copywriters simply don't have enough time to rework what they write, so that they can come up with the best texts and headlines possible.

Agencies, however, have a trick which enables them to produce consistently high responses, easily and effortlessly. . .

Think what you could do with such a trick, especially if you were an excellent copywriter to boot.

The trick that direct mail agencies use is this:

VARY YOUR OFFER!

Experience has proven, absolutely conclusively, that making a minor alteration in an offer can easily affect sales by 15, 30, 50 or even 100 per cent! For better . . . but also for worse!

How to change the offer in your headline

Experts like Jim Kobs (co-founder of one of the most successful direct mail advertising agencies) have managed to come up with over 100 variations on a single offer. We will look at just a few here.

- **Free trial period**
  Often with the added stipulation – 'Above all, do not send any money now!' This has become a pillar of direct mail sales.

- **Free gift if you write for more information**
  If the gift is really related to the product you want to sell, then not only do you avoid encouraging people who just want to get something for nothing and who will never buy your product, you also narrow down (qualify) your target group: the quality (customers who are already mail order buyers) of the addresses you receive will be more valuable you will also receive more demands for information than if you didn't offer a free gift.

- **Discount for cash payment (or payment in full)**
  This is the most traditional kind of offer, even though it may not be the best. Would you eat discount food or buy slightly inferior medication? Of course, it all depends on what kind of product or service you're offering, but as a general rule people associate discounted prices with inferior quality.

- **Special price due to . . .**
  Offer a special price to launch a new product, to do an annual clearing of inventory or slightly defective stock etc. Whenever you have a problem, share it with your clients – use the problem to explain why you're offering a reduced price. Never offer a reduction without providing a real – or at least plausible – reason for doing so. People like getting a great deal, but are also wary of offers that look too good.

And while we're on the subject of special offers, I should tell you that it isn't unusual for direct mail companies to damage their own products slightly, so that they can fill the demand for 'slightly damaged X's' which they offered in a 'Special offer due to. . .' campaign.

- **Special offer with time limit**
  A classic approach that often produces excellent sales, but which entails a good deal of risk: return your coupon within 48 hours, 10 days etc. It is a lot less effective when a set date (11 February, 25 June etc.) is used instead of a period of time (48 hours).

- **Sweepstakes**
  To organise a sweepstake, pick the winning numbers at random before any mailing or distribution is carried out. Then send your mailing with

the winning numbers included, to your target prospects or clients, along with your sales offer. When prospects receive their numbers, they may already be winners of the prizes you are offering. To find out (if they're winners or not) they have to return their number. Most people believe that if they don't order, they will not receive a prize. So most of them send their order together with their claim for a prize.

Here's the official definition. Sweepstakes work well when a lot of little prizes of insignificant value are offered alongside a limited number of 'major prizes'. The text should say 'You Have Won!' or 'Rub the box to find out if your number is a winner!'
Reader's Digest are the masters of the sweepstakes method.

- **Front-end load-up**
  This is another classic approach. You offer 'four books for only £20' or 'Buy two cassettes for £15 and get a third free!' The only condition is that clients buy another four books or another ten cassettes over the course of the following year.

Naturally, you can also combine approaches and make a number of offers at the same time.
Note that two offers combined produce better results than one, and three produce better results than two, four than three etc.
So, you should not only test the offers that seem best suited to your product or service, but also various combinations of offers: you're sure to come up with some pleasant surprises.
Depending on how it is formulated, an offer can produce mediocre returns . . . or it can go through the roof!
The famous story about the American book club that offered four books for a dollar is a clear demonstration of this phenomenon. Since this initially fabulous offer lost some of its effectiveness over time, a number of different headlines were tried to revive it. The one that worked best read: 'A book for only $1 PLUS 3 more free!
Actually, the offer was exactly the same – it was simply formulated differently.

How to find offers that produce high sales

Use the same procedure as you would for headlines.

- Try to 'infiltrate' the competition – make a conscious effort to read as much publicity as you can: buy things by correspondence instead of in shops; subscribe to a variety of magazines and newspapers; send in coupons for 'free trials' and 'special gifts'. Your name and address will quickly find its way on to a number of mailing lists, and the amout of so-called junk mail you receive will increase dramatically, providing you with even more food for thought.

■ Collect examples of offers. Use a drawer in a filing cabinet to store all the direct mail offers you receive, and all the interesting ads you've cut out of newspapers and magazines.

■ From time to time, study your collection. Criticise the various approaches, and take special notice of the changes made to a campaign between its first mailing and one sent out a few months – or even years – later. This can be very instructive. Next, sort your collection into categories, for example into different kinds of offers;

  – pay later;
  – free gift;
  – other 'free' offer;
  – discount;
  – special prices;
  – samples;
  – limited duration;
  – guarantee;
  – increasing the total value of the order;
  – sweepstakes;
  – 'clubs' for privileged clients;
  – special campaign.

■ Assign a number to each new offer in each of these 12 categories and then write down any ideas a new offer inspires you with.

In short, always be on the lookout for new, clever offers. And remember: **'A good offer is half the sale!'**

Increase your returns by 20 to 30 per cent or more!

This offer merits an entire volume of analysis. It is one of the most powerful tools available in direct mail sales, namely **'THE FREE GIFT'**.

On a symbolic level, receiving a gift means being recognised and is therefore an affirmation of the value of your existence.

On a psychological level, a gift represents much more than its market value: to a large extent it is perceived, by the beneficiary, as a personal sacrifice made by the generous donor.

Conclusion: a gift that costs you £3, but which allows your prospect to dream a little, will paradoxically be more important to that person than other gifts which cost £15, or £35 or even £75, and in some cases a lot more than that. So remember: a free gift can work magic!

In some cases, a copywriter can even transform a free gift into the main product, while the product that was originally offered becomes the supplementary item . . .

Make sure to indicate the words 'Free Gift' on the package. Direct mail prospects are often hesitant about accepting anything, fearing some kind of scam, or that they'll have to pay charges even though they didn't order anything etc. So do anything you can to reassure them, right from the start.

Also, as we've seen earlier, the words 'new' and 'free' are the two workhorses of direct mail advertising. So saying 'free gift . . .' is a lot better than just saying 'gift . . .'.

You should also respect a number of rules which will ensure that your 'free gift' is perceived as such (think of the times you gave someone a present they didn't like – what was supposed to be a joyous occasion became a painful experience). Your free gift should:

- be attractive and promising;

- have some relation to the main product;

- cost as little as possible, while retaining the greatest possible impact;

- be exclusive;

- be so interesting that it could be a product to sell by itself.

A professional secret – and how to get the most out of it!

I've saved the best for last.

This isn't an offer, although you could use it to make one.

You know that the first thing prospective clients read when they get your message is the headline. All right, now what do you think they read next?

If you don't know already, you're probably in for a surprise. The story below will give you a hint.

The director of the US Marines Officers Academy asked Rene Gnam, a seasoned old copywriter, to come up with a text that would get more people to subscribe to the Academy's magazine.

A superb text, quite obviously the work of Mr Gnam, was submitted to the Admiral's office for approval.

The Admiral replied:

'We cannot agree with the postscript included in your letter. An admiral would never go back on his word – or refuse to uphold a promise he has put in writing.'

Since the rest of the letter was approved, and the real objective was to recruit as many subscribers as possible, Mr Gnam insisted on keeping the postscript. He challenged the Admiral to a little test: half the mailing list would receive the letter without the indication P.S., but with the paragraph originally intended to follow the P.S. moved up to become the last paragraph of the letter, just above the signature; the other half would receive the original letter, including the P.S.

The Admiral's office accepted the challenge and the test was carried out.

Note that the original version (the one with the postscript) produced three times more subscriptions than the second version (the one without the postscript). And this occurred despite the fact that the rest of the letter was exactly identical! The only difference was the indication P.S.!

In his book *Secrets of Direct Mail Sales* (E.M.E., 2nd Edn, 1988) John P. Lehnish describes how researchers at Columbia University in New York conducted a study on visual behaviour. They used hidden television cameras to observe what people look at when they open an envelope which contains a message.

The subjects did not know that they were being observed. The results showed the following: a large majority of readers started by looking at the letter's headline, in order to find out the general subject; they then looked for the sender's name, company etc.; next, they read a couple of lines of the letter, after which they went directly to the signature, which leads into the postscript. The paragraph following the P.S. was therefore usually read before the rest of the letter.

That is why so many direct mail letters have a postscript. If the P.S. is interesting and well-written, readers will read the rest of the letter. Even if the letter is more than a page long, readers will turn to the end and read the P.S. before turning back to read the rest.

Surprised?

What this means, in practical terms, is that following your headline, you should devote the most time in writing an effective postscript. You should also ensure you have an attractive signature, but that is a lot easier to do – we'll discuss it in more detail below.

How to write a high impact P.S.

As we've said, free gifts are one of the most powerful tools in direct mail sales. The P.S. formula most often used consists of describing the

the free gift to best advantage and outlining the conditions required to receive it.

Here are some examples.

> **P.S. You can also get this FREE GIFT!**
> The Lucky Luke card deck, 54 brightly illustrated cards, available nowhere else. Spend hours playing with your kids – they'll love the colours and fun pictures drawn specially for you by Morris. Lucky Luke is the King, the Dalton gang are the Jacks, Ma Dalton is the Queen of Spades, Ran-Tan-Plan and Jolly Jumper are jokers!

This is a good example of how to 'sell' the gift to increase its value.

> P.S. This is just a reminder that your company will not have to pay the usual registration fee of £190, which I am pleased to offer as a **FREE GIFT!**

You can also set a time limit or deadline. This encourages prospects to respond quickly and therefore to read the rest of the letter right away.

> P.S. To get your name on the waiting list, I suggest you send us your return coupon as soon as possible.

You can also use the postscript to develop a 'last minute' argument – yet another reason for buying your product, which acts as the finishing touch and leads to a definitive decision on the part of your prospects to 'go for it!':

> P.S. Don't be a winner who throws away 25 or even 50 thousand pounds!

Finally, it is always advantageous to associate, or combine, different forms of postscripts. If you think this makes your postscript too long, just split it up into a P.S. and a P.P.S. You can even use N.B.:

- **P.S.**
- **N.B.**
- **P.P.S.**

A last bit of advice concerning your P.S: whenever possible, write the postscript out in longhand, or find a typeface that resembles longhand.

This will add a lot more power of conviction, give it a kind of urgency and immediacy; also consciously, or unconsciously, prospects will be flattered – they'll perceive your P.S. as a personal note . . .

How do you get your P.S. to look handwritten? Well, write it out by hand, using a black pen (even if you want it to appear in blue on the finished letter) and don't be too neat! Then just give the original to your printer and they will do the rest!

How to increase sales – with just your signature!

Let's get back to your signature.

- Does it look real?
- Is it printed in a normal colour?
- Does it contain imperfections?

Study the signatures on sales letters. Some can be immediately identified as fake. Others look more real. Others look so real you want to wet your finger and see if it smudges.

This is so important that I advise you to sign any mailings of under 3,000 copies by hand!

You may say, 'That's too much! Sign 3,000 letters by hand?'

Don't get excited – you can do it while talking on the phone, listening to music, or the radio or while watching TV. You can think about something else . . . The only danger is developing writer's cramp!

Signing letters by hand gives them an authentic, personal look which obliges prospects to read them, and to answer you. You'll see the difference in your sales! So keep in mind that 'the reward is worth the effort' and sign your letters by hand, whenever possible.

SUMMARY

- You can easily increase sales by finding variations of your offer.

- Combine successful offers to come up with the best one.

- A free gift is one of the strongest offers: offer at least one, and if possible two or three!

- Make sure your readers realise that your free gift has a much greater symbolic value than it's really worth.

- Take care to write a good P.S: this is what prospects read immediately after the headline.

- Pay attention to your signature: this is what readers look at right before the P.S.

· ·

CHAPTER 8

How to find effective ideas and arguments that sell

Put your most powerful idea-bank to work

Do you know where to find the largest interconnected network in the world? A network with so many connections, that if you had to write out the number using the same size characters as this book, you'd have to add a string of zeros more than ten miles long!

This network is also an amazing laboratory, which registers between 10,000 and 100,000 chemical reactions per minute.

I'll give you a hint: the network is enclosed in a kind of box and contains an average of ten billion cells . . .

The box, of course, is your skull and the fantastic laboratory/network is your own brain! And it's in this immense living laboratory that ideas are born. In fact, creativity is nothing more than the faculty of giving birth to ideas. And, once in a while, you'll come up with an idea that borders on genius, an idea with enormous commercial potential. In a laboratory as sophisticated as the one you have, this should be easy to do – as long as you know how to use it!

The human brain is composed of two parts, connected by an extremely complex system of nerves:

- the *left side of the brain* handles functions like language, logic, reasoning, analysis, space–time perception etc.;

- the *right side of the brain* is more intuitive and controls functions like rhythm, music, images, imagination, colours, dimensions etc.

Keep the difference between left and right brain functions in mind.

Coincidentally, there are also two types of creativity: one is based on reorganising bits of known information, thus creating new and different information which, however, is only an original way of combining known facts. This type of creativity is called synthesis.

Then there's the other kind, where ideas seem to surge up out of nowhere. This type of creativity is called intuition.

This is certainly the more noble of the two types of creativity, because it seems to materialise from nothing, bringing into being something that was not there before.

Intuitive creativity also usually precedes logical reasoning: you 'have a feeling about something' which isn't based on anything tangible or precise, on no discernible reasoning process – it's just your intuition . . .

All right, but how do you get these flashes of intuition?

A secret for discovering effective ideas and arguments that sell

When we look at how some copywriters have achieved brilliant success, how they got started and how they used their intuition to come up with great ideas, we can see that there's a lot less magic involved than we originally thought: somehow, these people are capable of seeing a little farther ahead and on a slightly larger scale. In other words, their vision is not as limited as most people's.

Do the following experiment: walk around a room, pick out all the objects that are red and try to memorise them. Ready?

Now try to visualise all the black or dark objects in the same room. Make a list of those you can recall. Now go back and check. You've probably forgotten quite a few. Why?

You were concentrating so much on the red objects that you didn't pay any attention to the others. The same thing happens with ideas: you are limiting your vision (actually you are being conditioned to limit your ideas – in other words, you are being manipulated).

You're like the frog who hops eagerly along, following a beam of light in the night, only to find himself in a sack full of other frogs who have followed the same light and who are all heading for the dinner table!

Is this just a question of luck? In your little experiment, a good copywriter, whose intuition has sometimes resulted in millions of pounds worth of sales, will recall at least some of the dark coloured objects. Why? Because a trained copywriter's intellect is aggressive and curious enough not to look only at what is obvious (i.e. the red objects), but also at what lies behind the obvious. And this is because copywriters train themselves to make use of both the right and left side of their brains at the same time.

You won't get any of them to admit this fact – it is, after all, a secret – but consciously or unconsciously, voluntarily or simply through habit, all the best copywriters use this technique. How can you make it work for you as well?

How to develop your creative copywriting to its fullest

The first thing you have to do is stimulate your 'natural' spontaneous creativity as much as possible. 'If I weren't as naïve as a child, I wouldn't be an inventor, states Roland Moreno, inventor of the well-known microchip for credit cards (and holder of 45 patents for this microchip, that brings Moreno over £150,000 in royalties every month, from all over the world!).

In fact, children have limitless imaginations. Unlike adults, they depend primarily on the right side of their brains, which is the seat of creativity.

How can you become as creative as possible? Well, it's a little like a child's game: the most inventive people are those who have retained a childlike curiosity which allows them to free their imaginations, to drift off and to escape into the world of dreams . . .

To help you regain this sense of childlike curiosity about the world around you, start by developing a conscious and confident relationship with your own subconsious mind.

- Make a conscious effort to recall all the occasions (at least three, whatever they may be) where you exhibited any kind of creativity (if possible, occasions where you 'amazed' yourself or the people around you). Try to relive the experiences in vivid detail, reviving the feelings of pleasure and accomplishment you felt, so that you build up a sense of confidence in your own creativity.

- Never force yourself to be creative. On the contrary, you have to be very relaxed for your imagination to function.

- Don't criticise yourself, don't judge yourself and, above all, don't judge the quality of the initial ideas that come to your mind.

- Next, get into the habit, a few times a day, of stopping your ~ interrupting the continuous process of analysis that occ~ Instead, just try to feel things and let your mi~ freedom.

Make an effort not to react like ~

98

Try it out for yourself – you'll be amazed at how well it works. It's almost magic!

Put your right brain to work!

Here's a concrete method, in four steps:

1. Enter information

When you prepare a sales letter or an ad for a given product, you should refer to a number of sources of information.

The first of these is your files.

Every time you see an interesting ad, cut it out. Every time you receive a sales letter, file it away. Classify all these documents according to subject.

For example, I keep seven files, each with a different colour, which corresponds to the following categories;

WHITE	personal development
YELLOW	money
ORANGE	book clubs
RED	sexuality
BLUE	weight loss/gain
GREEN	health
PURPLE	appliances and other miscellaneous items

This is good enough to start, but you should update your files as you gradually collect more and more material.

Each ad or letter is read and analysed, and any ideas they may inspire are noted and filed under the appropriate category.

Of course, to fill your files with information, you should subscribe to as many publications as possible and respond to all the direct mail offers you receive, including those from other countries.

The product itself

Study it. Use it. If it's a book, read it. You should know everything about the product. Talk to people who've used it or sold it before. Visit the factory or lab where it is made.

If the product is new – and you therefore don't have access to this kind of information – then test a similar product made by a competitor.

Other documents about the product

If the product has already been advertised elsewhere, study the publicity. Read any letters or testimonials submitted by satisfied – or dissatisfied – clients. Find out if any market studies were done, if there are any reports by consumer groups etc.

How to 'brainstorm'

Invite a group of interested people together and get them to brainstorm for you. Brainstorming was invented by one of the great names in advertising: Alex F. Osborn.

This method is based on the principle of 'differential judgement', which suggests that looking for solutions to a problem occurs in two separate phases:

- first, looking for possible solutions without any criticism at all, i.e. collecting ideas with a completely open mind;

- secondly, noting and evaluating all these ideas, the fruit of the collective minds of six to ten people (ideally) who are as different from each other as possible (in terms of education, cultural background, age, professional standing etc.).

Here are a few rules to follow.

1. **All critical judgement is withheld** – criticising the ideas is reserved for later.

2. **The craziest flights of imagination are welcome** – the more 'far out' or absurd an idea seems, the better; it's easier to bring a crazy idea 'down to earth' than to make an ordinary one 'fly'.

3. **Quantity is more important than quality** – the more potential ideas you have, the better your chances are of finding a 'great one'.

4. **Combining and improving ideas is highly recommended** – As well as submitting original ideas, participants are asked to express their opinions on how to combine and/or improve ideas suggested by others. In this way, someone's original idea may go through a number of transformations or variations. Ideas can also be combined, associated or fragmented to build new approaches.

Of course, during a brainstorming session everything must be taped or taken down by a shorthand secretary.

How else to channel creativity

You can also use other effective techniques for channelling creativity, such as: 'If this, then . . .'.

The principle of this technique is based on the game approach: 'If this, then. . .'. For example, if I reduce the weight of my product, then I can send out twice as many for the same price. You play with all kinds of ideas and try to visualise all kinds of possibilities in the hope of coming up with new approaches. You can also get a few people together for an 'If this, then . . .' session and apply the same rules as you would for a brainstorming session.

The discovery matrix

Developed by Abraham Moles, a specialist in communication, this technique consists of applying the approach of combining ideas in a systematic way. Using a graph, you can relate different elements which, at first glance, seem to have nothing to do with each other.

For example, say you're looking for ideas about new products because you want to expand your company's operations. The first step is to analyse the needs, expectations and dissatisfactions expressed by consumers. Then you analyse the capacity and technical expertise of your company, and try to put the two together. This will give you a 'need–possibilities' matrix.

In the following example the graph has been drawn up to think about the design of a beauty product:

Needs / Possibilities	Odourless	Bottle	Liquid	Design	Decoration
Financial					
Technical					
Marketing					
Sales					
Personnel					
. . . .					

Once the table is complete, each box is analysed and you ask the following questions:

- Is there a solution here?
- Are there any other more original or effective solutions?

An empty box means that no problems have been perceived. This is an innovative way to come up with great product ideas. Draw up your own discovery matrix and use it.

Scenarios

The principle here is to write as imaginative a description as possible of a situation that involves various problems.

In your ideal scenario, the problems are magically solved.

You'd also do a 'worst-case scenario' to help you avoid negative repercussions and prepare alternative plans to improve a bad situation.

Once the theme of a scenario is well defined, present it to a group (three or four people maximum) and ask for their comments, using sketches and tables as support documents. The challenge here is to transform the scenario into concrete suggestions for action.

2. Write a programme

Creativity is something that has to be practised and cultivated: first, through experience, namely the more you write letters, the easier it gets; secondly, through games.

a. For example, complete this series of letters:

OXXOXXOXXOX?

That was easy!

b. Here's one that's a little harder:

1 7 3 6 5 5 7 4 9?

c. Here's another classic creativity puzzle. Using a maximum of four straight lines, and without lifting your pen off the paper, join all the dots.

If you couldn't find the solution, it was because you were limited in thinking that your lines had to remain within the boundaries of the dots. And it often happens that the limits we impose on ourselves prevent us from finding solutions.

d. Here's a final creativity game: try to guess which sign is the logical progression of the following.

The answer is:

What comes next?

The answer is:

What's next?

The answer is:

And the next one?

Answer:

and the next are   And the one after that?

and then

Were you able to guess? I'll give you another hint. The next sign is:

|oo|

Solutions

a. X

b. 3

c.

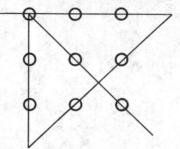

d. They are all symmetrical, composed of two mirror images of the other.

$$1\;2\;3\;4\;5\;6\;7\;8\;9\;10$$

We'll stop there, since this was not meant to be a book about games! But what conclusions can be drawn from these games and the difficulties you had finding the solutions?

- You have to be intellectually stimulated, at least to some extent, in order to find the solutions.

- You have to believe that there is a solution in order to find one. If you think the puzzle is a trap and has no solution, then you'll give up.

- You have to break out of the limits of conformity.

- The simplest things are not always obvious.

- Getting discouraged extinguishes creativity.

Psychological factors

These games suggest that one important factor for developing creativity is simply not to inhibit it by saying things like:

'I'll do better tomorrow . . .'

'I'm tired . . .'

'What are people going to think about me . . .'

'It's better if I don't take the risk . . .'

'I have to . . .'

'I shouldn't . . .'

'Anyway, I'm the kind of person who . . .'

'I'm content with what I've got . . .'

'I'm afraid of what I don't know . . .'

'I already know . . .'

'I've got a mental block . . .'

Get into the habit of replacing these kinds of discouraging thoughts with other, more positive ones. The trick is to 'empower' yourself – to authorise yourself to try something new. This isn't something that comes from outside. Creativity is something you already have inside you – all you have to do is free it.

Jean Cocteau (a famous French author/artist) said:

> 'Inspiration isn't something that falls from the sky. Rather, it is the result of a kind of profound indolence, and of our inability to reach certain forces deep within ourselves. These forces are always active, but it takes some exceptional event to awaken us from our state of somnolence and make us use them.'

Here are a few positive thoughts which you can use to stimulate your creativity:

'I am breathing . . .'

'I am vibrant . . .'

'I love myself . . .'

'I love you . . .'

'I sing . . .'

'I'm having fun . . .'

'I'm amusing myself . . .' (Think about the connection between 'amusing myself' and 'a muse', i.e. being your own muse!)

'I play (recreate) . . .'

'I let myself go . . .'

'I'm confident . . .'

'I dare to . .'

'I'm opening up . . .'

'I'm playing . . .'

You have to relax to be creative.

3. Ask a question

In order for your subconscious to work on its own and come up with solutions, you must give it a precise objective.

For example, 'Find the best title for the book I've just written on repairing home computers'.

Or better still, 'Find a catchy and convincing title'.

At the same time as you ask the question, set yourself a time limit. 'Now that I have all the information I need, I'll write the text of this ad next Friday morning at 9 o'clock'.

Choose the right time to programme your subconscious. Ideally, this would be when your subconscious and conscious minds are close to merging:

- just before going to sleep;

- while relaxing;

- when driving;

- travelling (on an aeroplane, boat, train etc.).

You'll get much better results if you choose the time carefully.

One of the most fascinating mental processes is called creative expectation. If you believe in what you're doing, if you have confidence that your creativity will produce results, then it will happen.

First programme yourself, then be confident.

4. Listen for the results

Even though you've set a date, your mental computer may start providing you with answers as soon as its work on the problem is completed, without waiting for the prescribed time. So you have to be in a state of readiness, pen and notebook at hand, and write down whatever thoughts you have. Keep a notebook in your bathroom, in the lavatory, next to your bed, in your car, on your person at all times etc.

Do not put off writing things down until later! As soon as a possible solution comes to mind, stop everything and write it down! If you don't, the chances are you'll forget it.

The power of the 'tree' technique

All right, you start getting more and more ideas. Some are interesting, some are even pure genius!

All this bubbling creativity is very nice, but you still feel that you're not doing the best you can. And you're right!

What you need is a method which you can use to channel your creative energy – to concentrate it and control it.

A young creative writing professor, Gabrielle Lusser Rico, teaching in San Diego University, found a way of applying recent clinical discoveries concerning the right brain to help make the process of finding ideas easier. Here's what he has to say:

> 'Right brain thinking is not organised in a linear way: it is random. So making a list is a kind of an aberration. To stimulate the right brain, ideas have to be represented as floating in space, somewhat like the way they appear in our brain. This led to the development of the tree diagram.'

You start by writing the central idea in the middle of the tree. You then write any subsequent ideas, stemming from the central idea, around it. You continue the process by adding smaller circles of ideas around those secondary ones and so on.

On the next page, you'll find an example of a tree diagram that starts with the central idea of 'memory'. You'll have to admit that the tree technique is a lot more productive than making an ordinary list. I found I got almost 30 per cent more ideas. Try it and see for yourself.

Note: if you run out of space and want to extend a 'branch', just use another sheet of paper. Use the secondary idea as a starting point and continue from there.

The most powerful method of transforming a good idea into a real success

I spent years training sales people, explaining to them that you always have to transform the characteristics of a given product into

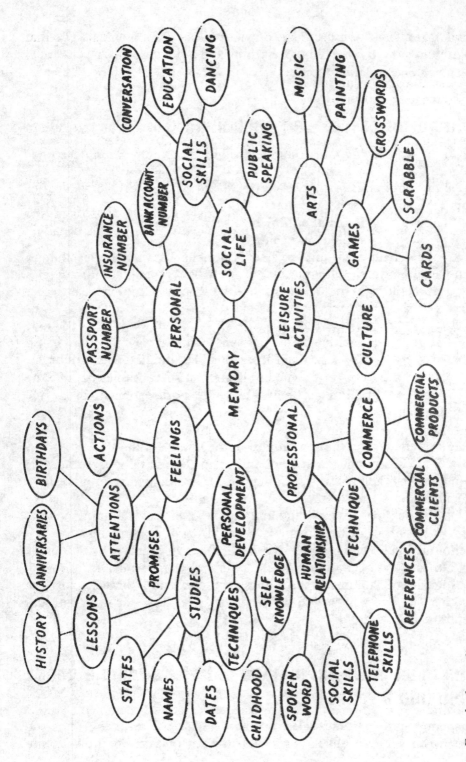

Example of a tree diagram.

advantages. But it wasn't until I began working in direct mail sales that I realised:

1. just how important this is;
2. to what extent it improves sales.

To reformulate ideas and transform them into advantages, all you have to do is follow the rules governing creativity: 'This reminds me of . . .'.

For example, say I'm selling a book on *How to do Better in Your Exams and Improve Your Study Habits*. It deals with things like memory, stage fright, learning exercises etc.

If I exchange places with one of my potential readers, I would ask myself the following question: 'What is this book going to do for me personally?'

Answer: the book can help me:

■ learn another language;

■ start using computers;

■ prepare for written or oral exams;

■ write a thesis;

■ control my fear of speaking in public.

If I then take the process a step further, and reformulate these advantages once more, we come up with something completely different:

Would you like to:

■ Speak another language?
■ Learn all about computers?
■ Get a university degree – and a better job – with ease?
■ Remain perfectly in control, even in the most stressful situations (meetings, oral exams, interviews, speeches etc.).

The main difference between the two versions is that the first talks about the effort required to achieve these things (which is not a great way to motivate people), while the second talks about results, i.e. what occurs after the effort is made.

People are much more highly motivated by thinking about the end result rather than about all the effort it takes to get there!

You have to become a master at reformulating your ideas in a positive way, so that they come across as advantages. Not only will this process provide you with a lot of new ideas and pertinent sales arguments (which was your original objective), you'll also find you get better at it as you practise. Your work will go more smoothly and provide ever greater sales.

The reformulation technique

I've saved the best for last. The code name is reformulation.

In fact, reformulating your ideas can completely change your perception of the product you're handling!

Every product has its characteristics. Some may even be remarkable. But the technical description of even the most remarkable product in the world is uninteresting (except to a technician).

On the other hand, if you can turn each of these characteristics into an advantage, then you have something people are interested in hearing about. This is the secret of reformulation.

Let's take a product, say an inflatable balloon that plugs into your car's exhaust pipe to inflate, and which you can then use to lift the car when you have to change a tyre. If you describe the product's characteristics to an average motorist, you'd probably get a response somewhere between 'You must be kidding . . .' and some vague interest, followed by doubts as to whether or not the thing really works.

Now, forget about characteristics, and start thinking about advantages, and you come up with a whole new set of ideas!

For example, you could say the following.

- The balloon inflates in just a few seconds and makes changing a tyre easier than ever. No wasted time, no missed appointments.

- It lifts the entire right or left side of the car – change a flat tyre, or replace summer or winter tyres in half the time!

- If you get stuck in mud or snow, just use the balloon to lift your car, and then slide a piece of wood, or some gravel, or branches under your tyres. You'll be out in no time!

- Because the balloon's surface is so large, it can be used to lift your car in places where a jack would be dangerous (soft ground, steep hill etc.).

- Keep a balloon in your boot and feel secure, wherever you go. No more worries about getting stuck or fixing a flat tyre. It's so easy – lifting the car requires no physical effort whatsoever.

Conclusion? If you select, concentrate and combine advantages, you end up with a product that appears to be *indispensable* to the average motorist – the same motorist who just a few minutes ago was completely indifferent!

Also, you'll notice that in addition to stimulating and sharpening your creativity, the 'reformulating' technique helps you discover a host of excellent ideas that you'd probably never have thought of without it.

SUMMARY

- The left brain is the seat of logic and reason. The right brain is the seat of imagination and intuition.

- To establish a direct line of communication with your subconscious, you first have to develop a conscious – and confident – relationship with it. A number of exercises have been designed to help you do just that. Practise them!

- Develop your curiosity as much as possible, in order to stimulate and improve creativity.

- One of the keys to success and coming up with great ideas is really believing that a solution exists.

- To get your right brain to work for you:
  1. store as much information as possible;
  2. programme your subconscious to perform a task (such as solving a problem, or finding new ideas . . .);
  3. ask your subconscious a precise question.

- Transform all your product's characteristics into advantages, by using the 'reformulation' technique.

CHAPTER 9

How to keep your prospects intrigued right from the start

How to avoid the wastepaper basket in the first 20 seconds

I don't mean to give you nightmares, but I need to remind you of a horrible vision: your letter, your beautiful mailing, in which you've invested so much money, time and effort, which you've put all your heart and soul into writing, using everything you know about copy-writing . . . this beautiful document is being *irresistibly* drawn to the rubbish bin.

From the mailbox to the bin – this fatal voyage can be short – very short indeed!

The only way to save your mailing: attract your readers' attention, of course (we've explained how earlier on), but above all hold their attention as long as possible. How?

Well, let's look at the first step: arousing and attracting your readers' interest. We've already seen how a headline includes a 'promise' which makes prospects want to keep reading, in order to find out how you're going to solve their problems, fulfil their desires, calm their fears etc. So your headline not only attracts attention, it also arouses an initial interest on the part of your clients.

Now your task is to maintain this interest, while getting your readers to move from the large, bold type of the headline to the smaller type of your sales letter itself. And not only do you want to maintain interest, you want to arouse it even more.

So, how do you keep readers excited, after they read the headline? How can you get them to read the rest of your text?

Before showing you the weapons you have at your disposal (and very effective weapons they are!), I'd like to introduce an extremely subtle but powerful ally. . .

Some people call it 'human nature', others refer to it as 'laziness' or 'natural inertia', but it doesn't matter what term you use.

Put a child, or even an adult, in front of a television set and play a video-tape of some successful adventure film (like *Indiana Jones* or *Romancing the Stone*). Let five minutes go by, then turn off the sound and the picture, and watch what happens . . .

You won't have to wait long for your viewer to protest most vociferously! Why? Simply because all human beings enjoy a good story. Tell someone an interesting story and they'll listen to the end. Time seems to pass very quickly when you're listening to a good story.

The objective is the same when writing a sales letter: capture your readers' attention, arouse their interest and hold it, if possible until they finish reading your letter . . .

You can rest assured that if your headline was good enough to attract their attention in the first place, then you've already won half the battle! This is because people naturally enjoy a good story and are always curious to find out what happens in the end.

So, once your headline has worked, you have a natural ally working for you – the force of inertia.

Now you can also equip this ally with certain weapons that will make it more effective. Here are the weapons at your disposal.

How to tell a thrilling story

Tell a story, pure and simple. It's the simplest and most natural way to get your message across, although it may not be the easiest. But if you're a good storyteller, and know how to arouse your listeners' curiosity and sustain it, you will score high marks.

Here's an example:

> Sunday, 28 December 1902. Three o'clock in the morning. A woman, her face full of anguish, awakens next to her sleeping husband. She lifts herself painfully out of the huge Renaissance bed, almost doubled over with nausea, and drags herself along the floor towards the lavatory. Her husband wakes up soon after, covered in sweat, breathing heavily. He struggles to get up, takes a few steps towards a closed window, but falls to the floor before he can reach it. In a last desperate attempt, the woman reaches for a bell cord that

would summon the servants. But she's too weak, she falls to the floor and loses consciousness.

In the shadows, a coal fire casts an eerie glow, still dispensing a breath of meagre warmth into the room.

The bodies were found the next morning. . .

If the subject identified in the headline held an interest for you at all, it would be very hard, because of the tremendous force of inertia at work on your mind, to stop reading at this point.

Objective attained!

Ask your prospective clients a good question

This is the technique most often used by copywriters, with classic openings like: 'Did you know that?'

'Did you know that a homoeopathic consultation generally lasts two or three times as long as an ordinary medical check-up?'

'Why do you think this is so?'

This statement makes readers extremely curious. It's almost as if you're challenging them to find the answer.

'If you could [insert one or a number of advantages], would you be interested?'

This is called the Bettger technique, after the person who invented it. It leads automatically to a positive response in readers ('Yes, of course I would. . .') and therefore immediately arouses their interest. It should then be relatively easy to sustain their interest, at least for a few paragraphs.

'Do you remember. . . ?'

Appealing to people's memories is also a good way to arouse interest, because it adds the emotional impact of the memory to their rational thinking process, emotions which are sometimes very strong and which serve to reinforce their interest.

Break some kind of news to your clients

No matter what we're interested in, we're always looking for news – information, hidden documents, revelations, results, discoveries etc. We don't sit around waiting for them, but when they do happen, we stop everything and listen. People are naturally curious.

So, if people stop to listen to almost any news, then imagine how strong the effect is when the news you break is about their particular sphere of interest and concerns them directly!

For example, say you've already bought a couple of books on health from a mail order company, or some products they offered for skin or hair problems; you then get a letter whose first paragraph is:

> Here's some great news for men and women who suffer from dandruff, itchy scalp, very dry hair and so on. This new product actually . . .

The chances are pretty good, unless you have to leave immediately to catch a plane or a train, that you'll read the rest of the letter.

Objective attained!

Get rid of your clients' bad memories for them

Maybe you have a way to soothe a certain kind of pain or get rid of a particular problem your clients have. Use this to formulate your headline.

The best way to do this is to recreate the unpleasant situation and then offer a solution. Doing so solicits an emotional response, which reinforces the analytical process of deciding whether or not the product is worth buying (very like providing positive memories).

For example:

> You have to speak in front of a group of people. Suddenly your throat goes dry, your vocal chords start tightening up, your thoughts wander all over the place.
>
> Someone compliments you on the way you look – all you can do is stammer some incomprehensible reply.
>
> People are looking at you – you blush and turn away.
>
> We've all felt this way at some time or other. . .

And if you, the reader, have felt this way, what do you think you're going to do after a psychological slap in the face like this – read the letter or throw it away? Read it, of course.

Objective attained!

Sum it all up!

Sum it all up for your readers: concentrate all your arguments in one paragraph and make their mouths water!
Example:

> Magic rituals unearthed after centuries . . . How to attract money . . . love . . . How to completely neutralise any kind of hate and protect yourself against any kind of aggression . . .

If these things concern you (and since you've been targeted to receive this letter the chances are good that they do), it would be very difficult for you to refuse an offer like this one and throw the letter away instead of reading it.
Objective attained!

Use testimonials

This technique is subtle in the sense that readers start to identify with the hero of the testimonial, through a psychological process of projection, and start feeling their reactions, motivations etc., as if they were their own . . .
Example:

> I have a confession to make. I love eating. I can't resist a delicious little snack now and then. The problem is, I have to watch my weight.
>   Imagine all the trouble I went through trying not to eat too much . . . resisting temptation day after day . . .
>   That's right, I said *went through*, because that's all behind me now – since I found the solution to my problem!

And there it is! If you are in any way concerned about overeating, then you're hooked – there's no way you're not going to keep on reading!
Objective attained!

How to develop your own technique

There's no reason why you cannot combine two or three of these techniques, or even invent one of your own! There really are no limits.
    There is, however, one golden rule and that is TEST and TEST SOME MORE!

The only way to become a great copywriter and get consistent results is to experiment, and then test your approach to see how well it works.

SUMMARY

- Keep this image constantly in mind: your letter, irresistibly drawn towards the wastebasket. The only way to save your letter from being discarded is to attract the attention of your readers immediately and hold their interest throughout.

- The most effective techniques for keeping readers on the edge of their seats right from the start are:
  - telling a story that has some suspense;
  - asking the right question;
  - breaking some 'news';
  - erasing unpleasant memories;
  - offering testimonials.

- Constantly test your techniques in order to make steady and lasting progress.

CHAPTER 10

How to convince people who can't make up their minds – and increase your sales

The truth is not always appropriate

Say you're selling a 'Stairmaster' fitness machine and you have a client who was able to improve his performance from five flights to 127 flights of stairs in just five days. You checked him out and what he says is absolutely true. However, if you tell people this in your sales letter, they won't believe it! On the other hand, if you say he went from five flights to 25 flights, then people will believe you . . .

Why? Simply because it sounds more realistic.

Also, pay special attention to a close relative of realism: coherence. Be careful about putting too many different documents in a single mailing, especially if they were written by different people! A discrepancy, no matter how tiny (a number, a date etc.) may seem very insignificant to you, but it can actually destroy an entire mailing! So be very, very careful what you include . . .

Always prove what you say – and do it more than once!

Use whatever proofs you want, but make sure they respond to the following questions.

- How do I know this proof is true?
- Where did this take place?
- Who says this is true?
- What right does this person have to make this statement?
- How did this happen?

Always look for new ways to prove what you say.

A guarantee can be your proof. An offer can also be your proof:

> This product works, and here's the proof: if you don't get results, not only will I reimburse you in full, I'll also send you a cheque for £200 to compensate you for the time and effort you spent trying our machine.

Use expert opinions

For example, get a well-known personality or an expert to state why they liked your product, and how it can help others. If possible, get a photograph of the person and put it above the statement.

You can also ask other users to give you testimonials about why they liked your product.

Finally, you can make a testimonial yourself. If what you say sounds credible, it can be just as effective as an impartial opinion.

What if you are targeting another business?

It's now time to look at a special branch of mail order marketing, called 'business to business' sales.

Heads of businesses – people who are used to making decisions – do not react the same way that other members of the public do. They are not motivated by the same things (the proof being that mail order professionals have quickly realised that they get far better results when addressing someone with a particular position or function, rather than just a name). Also, you wouldn't offer such people the same kinds of products, since they are often more technically oriented, more professional and better able to understand complicated, detailed descriptions.

Therefore, as a copywriter, you have to adapt your style to the product and to the target clientele. Your text should be much more informative, more rational and provide more detailed descriptions. Also, and above all, it should offer more proof to support the validity of what you say. The opinions of reputed professionals, institutions and well-known experts are of capital importance. Make sure you include them if you ever decide to get involved in this type of specialised mail order sales.

The power of the 'lift letter'

How do you convince the maximum number of hold-outs and increase your returns by 20 to 40 per cent? (Or how do you convince people who can't make up their minds *and* increase your sales by 20 to 40 per cent?)

A technique called the 'lift-letter' was long kept a well-guarded secret by its inventor, Paul Greystone, founder of Greystone Press. But as soon as it became known, it spread like wildfire. Thanks to a single eight by ten piece of paper, printed in two colours, and added to the contents of a mailing, direct mail entrepreneurs were able to generate 30 per cent more revenue!

And what's more, the letter was so easy to write: the basic principle being that a person, either known or unknown to the reader, but who holds a position which is hierarchically superior to the person who wrote and signed the original sales letter, adds his or her guarantee – a kind of seal of approval – to the product and the terms being offered.

This is why a lift-letter often has a picture of the signatory on it.

What should a lift-letter say? It's very simple. A lift-letter often starts something like this:

> Dear
>
> Really, you surprise me. I can't for the life of me understand why you decided not to try XXX.

This is followed by:

1. answers to the main objections (too expensive, I have no time for it, etc.);
2. reasons for trying the product immediately;
3. a reminder of the free gift;
4. reassurances of the validity of the guarantee.

In short, the aim of a lift-letter is to remove any objections or doubts readers may have even before they arise and reassure them with a personal guarantee from a second signatory, who holds a superior position to the first.

This is a classic. And there's more. Lift-letters are effective, not so much because of their text (in fact, they're usually folded in half, or even in four), but because of a single sentence printed on the exposed side, which reads something like:

> Don't read this unless you've decided not to respond to our offer . . .

Read this only if you've decided not to respond to our offer . . .

Please read this letter only if you've decided not to try XXX immediately . . .

What happens when you read this message? There are two possibilities:

1. either you already want to buy the product, but you are so intrigued that you read the letter anyway, in which case your decision to buy the product is reinforced even more; or

2. you don't really feel like buying the product, but you're finally won over by the additional arguments in the lift-letter.

Result? In both cases, you recover a percentage of 'solid orders' that you would otherwise have lost, probably without even realising it. And when these tenths of a percentage point of sales accumulate, they can make all the difference between mediocre and extremely profitable returns.

How to prepare your readers for action

Sacha Guitry, a French writer and actor who was renowned for being provocative, wrote: 'The women you haven't had are probably the ones you didn't ask!'

What Mr Guitry jokingly suggests really does apply to most situations in life: you have to know how to ask for things. In fact, knowing how to ask is often the key to success: ask any top salesperson or head of business!

The same thing applies to copywriters: *never* hesitate to *ask* your clients to *act*. Don't be afraid of sounding too forward, aggressive or impolite: experience has shown that people rarely perceive a straightforward demand that way. And you'll also be finding out about very subtle ways to ask your readers to act, so subtle that they'll find it difficult to refuse your offer. . .

On the other hand, if you don't tell your readers what they should do, the chances are they won't do it!

Golden rule number one: before making an explicit appeal to action, set the groundwork for your attack.

1. Summarise the advantages of your offer

This is the most traditional way of going about getting your clients to act. It corresponds to the equation:

$$\frac{\text{advantage}}{\text{price}} = \text{value}$$

The greater the value, the easier it is, because price is no longer an obstacle. This is also the moment where you might want to add yet another argument in favour of buying your product.

2. Reassure your clients

If you're going to offer a guarantee, this is the time to do it, because this is the moment when your prospective clients are afraid.

You can also resort to one, or a number, of the techniques we described earlier for reassuring your clients and convincing people who can't make up their minds. Your objective is clear: before going any further, you are asking your clients to make some kind of sacrifice and you must reassure them strongly that they will not lose out.

Only then can you get them to act.

Getting your clients to act

Here's a classic plan for concluding a deal:

Price
↓
Don't miss out on an opportunity like this one
↓
1. Do this 2. Do that 3. Fill out . . . put in envelope . . . mail it today
↓
Every day that goes by you lose . . .
↓
Act now
↓
If not, you may forget
↓
P.S. Free gift if you send your reply before . . .

The words used in this conclusive phase all point in one direction: *action*. Because if your clients do not act immediately, they never will. Keep that firmly in mind: in direct mail sales, it's now . . . or never!

We all know how it works: you put off filling out the order form for later and then you forget about it. You put the offer in a drawer and that's where it stays. You may want to buy the product after reading the sales letter, but if you don't do it right away, you'll find all kinds of reasons why you shouldn't buy it later on.

Words that trigger an immediate action

To incite readers to act, copywriters use a very specific vocabulary. Here are the results of a study of 75 sales letters and their conclusions. Words and phrases that scored the highest were:

Today   *26 times*
Don't miss out (on an opportunity like this)   *16 times*
Quickly   *12 times*
Return (your order form) as fast as possible   *9 times*
Hurry   *8 times*
Take advantage of this special price (of this special offer)   *7 times*
The faster you respond, the faster . . .   *4 times*
As quickly as possible   *4 times*
Post your order form quickly   *4 times*
Do it now   *4 times*
Answer right away   *4 times*
Can I expect your answer tomorrow?   *4 times*
Don't wait any longer   *3 times*
Take advantage . . . while it lasts   *3 times*
Do it quickly   *3 times*
To be sure you qualify . . .   *3 times*
Don't put off making your decision   *3 times*
I want to thank you for responding so quickly   *3 times*

These are some of the most common phrases, but there are other ways of inciting your clients to act.

Five more effective techniques for inciting clients to act

1. Set an expiry date

Don't put off making a decision. Unfortunately, I can't guarantee delivery of this jewel of a product if your order form is dated after midnight, 28 March 1995. So don't wait! This is really a unique and rare opportunity!

2. Set a time period

I tried to spread this offer out over a period of time, so that we could serve you better, and so that Catherine, my secretary, would not get too overloaded trying to fill too many orders all at once. If you would be so kind as to mail your order within the next five days, I'd be happy to send you a little gift, as a token of my appreciation and friendship – a 'high performance' audio-cassette. So take advantage of this limited offer by sending us your order form today!

3. An imminent event . . .

Which may cancel out all or many of the advantages you've just offered, such as:

- a limited number of clients;

- running out of stock or an imminent increase in price;

- a special introductory price (launching the product, subscription drive etc.).

4. Offer a free gift *if* the client responds quickly

5. A list of everything the client has to lose . . .

By not responding quickly, or by passing up your extremely attractive offer.

Which technique is best?

Try to associate and combine a number of techniques, so that together they are perfectly suited to the type of product you're offering. In this way, the advantages of each single technique are multiplied (the whole is greater than the sum of the parts!).

Finally, tell your clients exactly what they have to do and do everything you can to make it easy for them.

For example, tell them explicitly to fill out the order form, to put it in the return envelope along with their cheque or credit card details and to drop it in the post-box. You must do this even though it may seem infantile and unnecessary, a little like talking to a child.

Telling them exactly what they have to do saves time since clients don't have to ask themselves all kinds of questions and it reinforces your original point: 'This really is easy!' In fact, you kill two birds with one stone: clients don't make any mistakes and you administer what is called 'The Lancaster Touch . . .'

Summarise the advantages

Lancaster was an American insurance salesman who discovered a pretty astute technique for making a lot more sales than any of his colleagues.

Towards the end of his presentation, after explaining and making sure the prospect understood everything, he would summarise all the advantages of his offer ('I believe I already told you that . . .') and made sure he got the prospect to respond with a 'Yes' answer to two or three very minor questions. He would then start filling out the contract as if it were the only natural thing left to do . . .

After completing the contract, he would offer his pen to the prospect and point to the place where the prospect was to sign.

And that's all there was to it! By some seemingly miraculous process, the number of prospects who actually signed was astounding.

Why? Because Lancaster did everything he could to make it easy for them: signing became the logical next step! Prospects understood this logic, and consequently asked themselves fewer questions and had fewer doubts. The transition from passive listener to activer buyer became completely natural . . .

You, too, can use the 'Lancaster Touch': prepare the groundwork, make things as easy as you can for your clients and lead them through a logical progression towards your objective – buying your product and sending you a cheque in the mail!

SUMMARY

- You have three ways to convince people who can't make up their minds;
  - formal, believable and coherent proof;
  - expert opinion;
  - the lift-letter.

- To get your prospective clients to act immediately:
  - prepare the necessary groundwork so that action is easy;
  - reassure them (with a guarantee if possible);
  - use 'trigger' words and phrases;
  - set an expiration date or time limit;
  - announce some imminent event (raise in price etc.);
  - offer a gift for responding quickly;
  - list all the ways they would lose out by not responding;
  - tell them exactly what they have to do.

CHAPTER 11

How to keep your readers reading – from beginning to end

It's a bit like football: after the kick-off (writing your headline) and the kick-off return (your letter's first paragraph) the objective is to score points!

How to make all of your letter exciting

Here's what you want to do: get your message across *and* hold your readers' attention, keeping them on the edge of their seats (panting for more).

Remember the comic books you read as a child? If you take a close look at the end of each page, and especially at the box in the bottom right-hand corner, you'll see that the writer/artist almost always breaks off at a point of suspense, which, of course, makes you want to turn the page and keep reading.

This technique has a very practical origin: comics were first published in newspapers and appeared a page at a time. Artists are still using the technique today, simply because it's a great way to capture and maintain the interest of their avid fans.

Take a look at a thriller or murder mystery. At the end of each chapter, you'll almost always find a question, a point of suspense, a crisis. For example:

'She hung up first. I stepped out of the phone booth, and that's when it all started.'

'I had absolutely no doubts about what really went on in Arizona while I was away.'

'Four hours later, I was on a plane heading for Europe. Heading for – and there's really no other way to put it – the biggest mistake I ever made.'

'She was gone for 11 days in all. Now she's back. And now it starts . . .'

But what about a sales letter? Well, it's very simple. You can use exactly the same technique to boost your readers' attention.

In the body of the letter itself, use any of the techniques we've already described to attract attention:

- ask a question;
- break some exciting news;
- summarise what you've already said.

You can also use the following techniques.

- **Puzzles/riddles** Any unusual or striking idea, anything intriguing which makes people want to know more . . .

- **A strong promise** Readers will ask themselves how you're going to keep it . . . and will continue reading to find out!

- **A new piece of information** It's up to you to develop ways to introduce some breathtaking news, but here are some lead-ins you can use to start:

  - And that's not all . . .
  - And it gets even better than that . . .
  - Wait a minute, the best is still to come . . .
  - But first, you should know about a few facts . . .
  - Now I'm going to show you why. . .
  - Now – and this is the most important part . . .
  - Now you will understand why. . .
  - But there's still one thing you have to do . . .
  - You may be asking yourself . . .
  - As you no doubt already know . . .

But boosting interest on its own isn't enough! You still have to make your readers *want* to move on to the next paragraph!

How to get your text read and understood, and obtain maximum results

An organisation called Chilton Research conducted a study of 100 magazines in order to find out how advertising text is read.

On average, the results showed that:

- 64.4 per cent of people saw the header and headline, and read them;
- only 24.4 per cent started to read the text; and
- only 13.7 per cent read more than half the text.

This means that more than 80 per cent of potential readers were lost.

How to multiply the numbers of your readers

Unfortunately, the same statistics apply to your texts. Whether you're trying to sell one of your products, or convince people to act, you lose most of your chances for success along the way. If your arguments are not read, it doesn't matter how good they are, they'll still have no effect.

To make your sales texts, business letters or information manuals work for you, it is essential that you master the rules of readability.

The opposite of what you learned in school

Mastering the rules of readability becomes all the more crucial in light of the fact that they are more or less exactly the opposite of the way you learned to write in school. And the further you got in your studies, the more handicapped you are!

But don't be alarmed – you're not the only one to suffer from this problem, and numerous researchers have already identified the causes, and their solutions. They noticed that texts that sell, books that are successful and magazines with large circulations, have certain factors in common.

Apply these common factors when writing your own texts and you'll be three, four or five times more effective than you are now. Let's look at what *stops* people reading and what makes them want to read to the very end.

What factors stop people from reading on?

To understand what turns your readers off, you must accept the following idea:

> **It's not up to them to make any effort whatsoever to render your text as easy as possible to read.**

People read in what are called 'spans'. A span is that part of a word or sentence which can be absorbed at a single glance and retained for a few moments.

If the reader is cultivated and highly educated, their span is large. If they are less educated, the span will be smaller. Some people's spans are so small that they practically have to decipher a text letter by letter.

The longer a sentence is, the harder it is to read

Your reader is like someone trying to guess what is inside a room by looking through a keyhole. It becomes all the harder to guess if:

1. the room is very large and complex (equivalent to long, complex sentences using difficult words);

2. the keyhole is very small (equivalent to a reader's limited intellectual capacity, resulting in very short spans).

Present your text so that it is inviting to read

Look at the piece of text below, labelled A. Would you say that the text is inviting? Is it easy to get into? No, of course not. It looks like a compact mass of words, which repels rather than attracts a reader's attention.

Now look at the next piece of text, labelled B. The short paragraphs make it much more inviting. It's always easier to digest small bits of information, one after the other, than an enormous amount all at once.

The arrangement of paragraphs can also affect the same sales letter. Version A uses long paragraphs:

Version A

When we examined 12 men suffering from urethritis (a painful disorder of the urethra) we discovered that there was no aggravation of the infection, or any damage likely to cause pain, during and after micturation. We then treated each patient with a combination of ordinary vitamins, administered orally, for four days. Result? Total remission of all symptoms.

The patient, a brilliant business woman, had already undergone three operations to soothe her back pains. When we were called in, she was already in the hospital again, on the point of having another, even more serious operation: an incision in her spinal cord which was

131

supposed to isolate the painful set of nerves. But before resorting to this Draconian procedure, her doctors wanted to try something different (the natural healing method described below). And, luckily, it worked! Today, she is in excellent health. She has no trouble walking or standing, takes no medication, doesn't suffer from insomnia or back pains, and has fully resumed her professional activities.

Read about all these actual cases before making up your mind to buy this work – an indispensable book! How can it help you? In countless ways! See for yourself! The first case of multiple sclerosis treated by Dr Kaslow concerned a patient who was incapacitated to the point of not being able to get up, dress or even feed herself. After a period of natural treatment (described below), using no medication, she was able to take care of herself once again, walk without a cane and this without recourse to any special remedy.

He cured cases of cystitis with an 85 to 90 per cent success rate, in three weeks to a month (sometimes a little more, sometimes less). And that's only the beginning! You still haven't heard about these amazing cases: a woman had such severe dizzy spells she was hardly able to stand up. The level of triglycerides in her blood was also very high. After three weeks on a diet designed specifically for her condition, her triglyceride level dropped 50 per cent and she experienced no dizziness whatsoever.

According to Dr Gorney, a more natural diet and lifestyle (see below) can produce astonishing results in cases of cardiac disease. Patients were . . .

When the writer realised how dense and unappealing his text was, he shortened the paragraphs. Obviously this required more space, but isn't it better to print another page and have your text read, than save a little paper . . . only to have it thrown straight into the wastebasket?

Version B

When we examined 12 men suffering from urethritis (a painful disorder of the urethra) we discovered that there was no aggravation of the infection, or any damage likely to cause pain, during and after micturation. We then treated each patient with a combination of ordinary vitamins, administered orally, for four days.

Result? Total remission of all symptoms.

The patient, a brilliant business woman, had already undergone three operations to soothe her back pains. When we were called in, she was already in the hospital again, on the point of having another, even more serious operation: an incision in her spinal cord which was supposed to isolate the painful set of nerves.

But before resorting to this Draconian procedure, her doctors wanted to try something different (the natural healing method described below). And, luckily, it worked!

Today, she is in excellent health. She has no trouble walking or standing, takes no medication, doesn't suffer from insomnia or back pains, and has fully resumed her professional activities.

Read about all these actual cases before making up your mind to buy this work.

It is an indispensable book! How can it help you? In countless ways! See for yourself!

The first case of multiple sclerosis treated by Dr Kaslow concerned a patient who was incapacitated to the point of not being able to get up, dress or even feed herself. After a period of natural treatment (described below), using no medication, she was able to take care of herself once again, walk without a cane and this without recourse to any special remedy.

He cured cases of cystitis with an 85 to 90 per cent success rate, in three weeks to a month (sometimes a little more, sometimes less).

And that's only the beginning!

You still haven't heard about these amazing cases:

A woman had such severe dizzy spells she was hardly able to stand up. The level of triglycerides in her blood was also very high. After three weeks on a diet designed specifically for her condition, her triglyceride level dropped 50 per cent and she experienced no dizziness whatsoever.

Apart from being more attractive, the second text can also be read much more quickly. A study conducted by Miles A. Tinker and Donald G. Patterson showed that a text with six times as many pargraphs is read 7.3 per cent faster.
And since your readers are probably in a hurry . . .

How long should your lines be?

Remember that each person has a particular reading span. If a line is too long, it becomes difficult to follow and comprehend. Inversely, if a line is too short – shorter than the reader's span – the fact of having to move to the next line breaks the train of thought.

A French researcher, Francois Richaudeau, demonstrated that lines which are too short (40 characters, including spaces) are actually more difficult to read than longer lines.

Miles A. Tinker and Donald G. Patterson found that lines of less than 22 characters, or more than 112 characters, slow reading down by five per cent.

Conclusion:

1. Avoid paragraphs that are too long. In a sales letter, for example, paragraphs which are longer than six lines – or more than 80 words – are considered too long.

2. Write your text (or get it typeset) in lines of between 50 and 80 characters (counting spaces). This is a good average.

How to cut a paragraph

Normally a paragraph contains a single, unified thought, so cutting it means destroying its unity. But every idea is built on a collection of smaller thoughts and you can use these as transition points from one paragraph to the next.

For example, here is a paragraph written by Professor Siegfried Vogele which contains more than 14 lines. Can you cut it?

> The people who receive our promotional material read compulsively. They will only read a text if they see an advantage in it for themselves. To make this advantage obvious to them, the language we use has to be simple and comprehensible. And this is especially true if our target audience is a general cross-section of the population, which of course represents the largest segment of the market. If we send these people offers which are too difficult for them to read and understand, we considerably reduce our chances for success. Anyone who is aware of this and still makes no effort to make it as easy as possible for readers to understand a text, should not be surprised if their endeavours result in failure.

Where should you cut?

Ideally, you'd cut somewhere in the middle of the text, so that the remaining paragraphs still have some substance.

What do you think? Should we cut after the word *comprehensible*? Or after the word *market*?

I think it would be hard to cut the paragraph after *comprehensible* because the next sentence – *And this is especially true if our target audience. . .* – is directly related to the previous one. On the other hand, the link between the following two sentences is more artificial.

Since each paragraph should be able to stand alone, you may have to modify the text to some extent. In our example, the phrase '*If we send these people . . .*' links the sentence to the previous one. But if you change '*these people*' to '*your prospective clients. . .*' the link is less apparent. This would give us:

> . . . represents the largest segment of the market.
>
> If we send our prospective clients offers that are difficult to read and understand, we considerably reduce our chances for success.

As you can see, the second sentence now contains a complete thought and can therefore be isolated, while in the first version it was linked to the previous sentence.

Let's try another one. This text by Francois Richaudeau has more than 22 lines. Can you cut it into three paragraphs?

> Slow readers who analyse word by word rather than letter by letter, decipher an average of two words (11 characters) per glance, which corresponds to an average of about 100,000 characters per hour. As we have seen, fast readers can double or even quintuple this figure, and still usually retain more than slow readers. But in terms of instant vision, measured with the aid of a tachistoscope set at 1/1000, 1/50 or 1/25 of a second, we observed that fast readers did not decipher any more characters than slow readers – an average of between 15 and 20. This seems to confirm what we have stated about the mental nature of the reading process. To improve performance and help people read more quickly, we can use two 'black box' methods to mask the process.

Answer

We could cut the paragraph after '. . . *retain more than slow readers . . .*', which would give us:

. . . retain more than slow readers.

But in terms of instant vision, measured with the aid of a tachis-toscope set at 1/1000, 1/50 or 1/25 of a second, we observed that . . .

We could cut again after '. . . *the mental nature of the reading process . . .*'. This would make the last sentence an independent paragraph.

Don't be afraid of paragraphs that contain only one sentence

Henry Cowen, one of the highest-paid advertising writers in the world, and the originator of the 'Sweepstakes' concept, told me that he always got his best results from letters which started with very short paragraphs – one or two lines at most.

Here is an example of one of these letters:

To American Express Cardmember. . .

Writing very short sentences at the start of a text is a little like serving hors-d'oeuvres before a meal – they're easy to read and absorb, and stimulate the reader's 'appetite' for the main course – the longer para-graphs that follow.

It's also a good idea to use a one-sentence paragraph in the middle of a text, in order to recapture the reader's attention. If you ask a question, for example, 'Are you wondering about the price?', isolate it by making it a whole paragraph.

John Caples, one of the greatest copywriters of our time, offers this advice, 'If you have an important sentence that you want to emphasise, you can get it to stand out by making it a whole pargaraph, sandwiched between two longer paragraphs.'

But everything we've just learned only serves to whet your reader's appetite. How can you make your entire text as easy to read as possible? That's what we're going to discuss now.

The longer your sentences, the less readers retain what they need

Long sentences are not only difficult to read, they're also difficult to retain.

In his book *Readability* (published by Retz) Francois Richaudeau pro-vides the following results of a study of fairly slow (and therefore average) readers:

Number of words per message	Number of words retained
12	100%
13	90%
17	70%
24	50%
40	30%

This means that a sentence of 24 words loses 50 per cent of its effectiveness!

The length of sentences can provide us with a pretty good idea of the kind of material we're looking at, as well as its target audience:

Cartoons	8 words per sentence
Romance novels	12 words per sentence
Women's magazines	14.5 words per sentence
Reader's Digest	16 words per sentence
Newspapers	18.5 words per sentence
Highbrow magazines	22.5 words per sentence
Scientific reports	29 words per sentence

How to shorten long sentences

If you think a sentence is too long, how can you make it more 'digestible'? Well, it's really very simple. Read the following example:

Doctor Javal, who in 1879 became the first person in France to study the physiology of reading and writing, and who discovered the jerky way the human eye moves across a page, came to the following conclusions about the readability of printed material.

1. Start by making sure you grasp the meaning of the sentence – read it over a few times.

2. Look for conjunctions – those famous little words like but, and, or, thus, neither, since, because etc. You can cut a sentence wherever the word 'and' appears, 90 per cent of the time.

Simply replace the 'and' with a full stop.

In this example, the word 'and' appears twice: the first in '. . . reading *and* writing . . .' and the second in '. . . *and* discovered . . .'. The first would be difficult to replace with a full stop, while the second is not.

But, this isn't enough. If you replace the second 'and' with a full stop, the sentence that follows becomes incomprehensible.

> Doctor Javal, who in 1879 became the first person in France to study the physiology of reading and writing. He discovered the jerky way the human eye moves across a page, came to the following conclusions about the readability of printed material.

Why is it incomprehensible? Because there is an unnecessary word (*who*) in the first sentence, and because the subject of the last verb in the second sentence (*came to*) is at the beginning of the first sentence (*Dr Javal*). So, we have to make another cut, transforming our initial sentence into three shorter sentences:

> Doctor Javal, in 1879, became the first person in France to study the physiology of reading and writing. He discovered the jerky way the human eye moves across a page. He came to the following conclusions about the readability of printed material.

Not bad, but not very pretty either. The two '*he's*' are clumsy. You could improve it somewhat by saying: '. . . *and writing. He was the one who discovered . . . and came to the following conclusions about . . .*'.

Your turn!

Try to cut the following sentence:

> You are one of the lucky winners, that much is already certain, and the VIP card you received today, as well as your entry form for the many prizes we have to offer, are proof of that.

Your answer:
That's right, the easiest thing to do is replace the '*and*' with a full stop.

> You are one of the lucky winners, that much is already certain. The VIP card you received today, as well as your entry form for the many prizes we have to offer, are proof of that.

But you can go even further and make the second sentence more dynamic. Go ahead, give it a try!
Answer:

Do you want proof? Take a look at the VIP card you received today, and at your entry form for the many prizes we have to offer.

Or:

You are one of the lucky winners, that much is already certain. Do you want proof? Look at what you received today:

- A VIP card
- An entry form for the many prizes we have to offer.

Changing the order of words in a sentence

When a sentence is too long and hard to understand, you can simply change the order of the words to make it easier to read – and more dynamic.

By showing you how to evaluate each of the functions of your business (from managing after-sales service, to production and administration) *Audit and Control Business Management* helps you strengthen the weakest links in your chain of command immediately, and avoid hazardous operations.

Cut this sentence as much as possible.
Sample response:

Audit and Control Business Management helps you strengthen the weakest links in your chain of command immediately, and avoid hazardous operations.
How?
By showing you how to evaluate each of the functions of your business, from production and administration to managing after-sales service.

Ready for another try?

According to the law, it is not permissible for all three legally protected organisms to be identical, since the controlling organism can be neither a member of the administrative body, nor employed by the company.

Go ahead.

Sample response:

> According to the law, it is not permissible for all three legally pre-
> scribed organisms to be identical. In fact, the controlling organism
> can be neither a member of the administrative body, nor employed
> by the company.

You can even cut the second sentence:

> In fact, the controlling organism can not be a member of the adminis-
> trative body. Nor can it be employed by the company.

Ready for another one?

> He summarises various theories about the typographical readability
> of the initial text for readers, and reviews the most significant studies
> which support and lend credibility to these theories.

Take your time . . .
Sample response:

> He summarises various theories about the typographical readability
> of the initial text for new readers. Certain studies support and lend
> credibility to these theories. He reviews the most significant of
> these.

As you can see, it is fairly easy to cut sentences down to more readable size.
It's just a question of practice. The more you do it, the easier and faster it
becomes.

Influence of the spoken word

Listen to people around you talking – the sentences they use are very short.
The same goes for radio and television. Our civilisation is in the process of
making sentences shorter and shorter. And effective written language is
getting closer and closer to the spoken word.

This is even more true when you're trying to convince people. The
shorter your sentences are, the easier they are to understand. And the
better people understand your arguments, the more they will tend to think
like you and be persuaded to do what you want.

To sum up: paragraphs should be short, lines of average length and sentences short (unless you happen to be addressing a group of college lecturers). Are there any other factors which will help get your text read, understood and retained from beginning to end?

Yes. In fact, we still haven't talked about the two most important ones . . .

The shorter a word, the stronger it is: why?

Take a moment to think about the words that describe parts of your body: head, foot, leg, hand, eye, ear etc. They are all *short* words. Now think about the following words:

- oto-rhino-laryngologist;
- phenomenology;
- proportionality;
- incriminatory etc.

According to Rudolph Flesch, a pioneer in the study of readability and effective language, 'The more abstract the idea being expressed, the longer the word.'

Some readers have trouble deciphering long words because their 'span' is too short. In addition, it's as if a little alarm bell goes off in people's minds: 'Watch out! Difficult word ahead!'

Long words slow reading down

Francois Richaudeau measured the difference in reading speed of words with an average of 5.2 letters and a text composed of words with an average of 7.4 letters.

Result?

Average reading speed for the first text was 27,400 words per hour; for the second, 21,400 words per hour.

The law of least effort

That's a difference of 22 per cent! And, according to the law of least effort, if your text is in any way hard to read, people will tend to throw it away altogether or at best take a quick look at it.

If you examine the words used most often, for example the 1,300 most common words in the English language, you'll find they average between five and six letters per word. Not more!

Eliminate 'filter' words

A German researcher, Professor Siegfried Vogele, conducted a lengthy study of this phenomenon, especially related to commercial correspondence. In his experiments, he used cameras with extremely fast shutter speeds to examine the movements of the human eye.

According to Professor Vogele, words of one or two syllables (between five and six letters) *reinforce* reading, while longer words *inhibit* reading, acting as a kind of *filter*. Filter words eliminate a percentage of readers.

Completely getting rid of filter words produces the best results. However, at times the clarity of the text may suffer, since there may be no adequate shorter substitute for a long word. In such cases, a commercial text may have to use a word of four syllables or more. But there is a limit to how many of these exceptions readers will tolerate. The figure is between five and ten per cent, maximum. If there are between five and ten filter words in a 100-word text, the material is still readable, but only just so:

1. all long words (four syllables or more) above the ten per cent cut-off point *must* be replaced;

2. words of two and three syllables can sometimes be simplified.

How to shorten words

There are two techniques you can use to replace long words with shorter ones.

1. Find a synonym

Many word-processing programs come with a built-in dictionary of synonyms. All you have to do is select a word that is too long, enter a command and, hey presto, you are presented with a list of possible replacements. All you have to do is choose one and enter another command to carry out the substitution.

If you don't have a word-processor, you can use a printed dictionary of synonyms, such as *Roget's Thesaurus*.

Here are some examples. Try to find shorter words for the following:

construct;	incapacitate;
however;	apprehension;
unaesthetic;	sufficiently;
additional;	recreation.

These words can be replaced by:

construct – build;   incapacitate – hurt;
however – but;   apprehension – fear;
unaesthetic – ugly;   sufficiently – enough;
additional – more;   recreation – play.

2. *Replace one long word with a number of small words*

If you can't find a shorter synonym, you can paraphrase.

- Instead of *oto-rhino-laryngologist* write 'ear, nose and throat doctor'.
- Instead of *proportionally* write 'spread out fairly'.
- Instead of *temporarily* write 'for a short time'.
- Instead of *located at*, just write 'at'.

This applies especially to commercial texts.

As Professor Vogele remarked: 'This requirement applies only to advertising texts, sent to readers without their having asked for them.'

Obviously, people will make more of an effort to read texts they've bought and paid for, like books or magazines.

All the tricks you need to know to make a letter, word, sentence or paragraph stand out!

<u>Underline</u> important words or passages:

- by using continuous underlining;
- or by underlining separate words to create a staccato effect which creates an impression of urgency!

However, be careful not to abuse underlining: if you don't underline more than ten words per page (say five blocks of one to three words each), then a reader's eye will be unconsciously guided to these 'attention-grabbers' and use them as focusing points.

Result? You can *direct* your reader's eyes through the entire letter! This is a scientific fact, supported by all kinds of testing. So it's up to you to make judicious use of the technique . . .

You can also use other kinds of focus points:

points, asterisks, blobs and colons of various sizes

arrows (resembling hand-written ones if possible).

Place these in the margins to indicate an important line or paragraph, or to list a number of advantages.

Juggle your formats

Think about the way you begin your most important paragraphs (two per page maximum): you can indent or not, have them flush right instead of flush left, enclose them in a box etc.

Note: do not use unusual colours! Tests have shown that you will always obtain the best results by having your text printed in black, and any underlining, footnotes, signatures etc. in blue.

You can use red, but only for a very few paragraphs (if you can afford to print in three colours!).

Transitions

Make regular use of transition phrases or words that keep people reading. For example:

In effect	Since
Thus	Immediately
For example	Next
Whoever	Another
Therefore	On the contrary
Now that	Finally
In addition	A second point
Of course	On the other hand
Finally	The same applies to
In fact	Here
Here	Despite
And	In the same way
Once again	In other words
And there you are	Or

Which typefaces should you use?

Don't change typefaces more than twice in your letter itself. Characters with a serif (for example Times or Plantin) are easier to read than characters without a serif (for example Univers or Helvetica). Keep 'sans serif' typefaces for headings, or when your copy is very short.

If you really want something to stand out, use *italics* or a **bold** face. Use 'attention-grabbers'.

Make regular use of words and phrases that intensify your readers' interest. For example:

- To be honest, really, just between you and me, etc. . . Such phrases have the advantage of adding a personal, intimate, sincere and honest touch to your text, improving your relationship with your prospective clients.

- And that's not all. . . People want to know what more you could possibly add to your offer. A surprise? A free gift? They'll keep on reading to find out.

One more trick: avoid starting a paragraph with an article (a, the, these, those etc.). You're always better off trying to capture your readers' attention and interest right from the start, so don't use colourless, uninteresting words to start a new paragraph.

How to keep your readers turning the pages

Here again there is a very simple, yet effective way to keep readers turning the pages of your letter. The technique can also be used at the bottom of a column, to get readers to move on to the next column. Here are some examples:

- `You can expect a surprise. In fact ...`

                                                            PTO

- `And above all ...`

                                                            PTO

- `And there's a lot more than that ...`

                                                            PTO

- `Now I'm going to prove that this is true ...`

                                                            PTO

- `By using this appliance over the next couple of months, you'll be saving up to ...`

                                                            PTO

145

Sales Letter Checklist

Date: Title: Author:

Element Analysed	Score (circle a score between 0 and 500)					Comments and advice	Score
HEADLINE	Doesn't work 0	Works a little 100	Average 250	Works well 400	Works very well 500		
HEADLINE DESIGN	Unreadable 0	Slightly readable 5	Readable 10	Well designed 15	Very readable 20		
PROMISE/CURIOSITY	Very weak 0	Weak 10	Average 20	Strong 30	Very Strong 40		
LETTERHEAD/LOGO (may also appear at the bottom of the page)	Amateur 0	Not developed 5	Not bad 10	Inspires confidence 15	Suits the product 25		
OPENING PARAGRAPH	Boring 0	Incomplete 5	Average 10	Interesting 20	Captivating 30		
OFFER	No offer 0	Unclear 10	Average 30	Good 50	Excellent combination 75		
ADVANTAGES	None 0	Few 5	Needs development 10	Well developed 20	Very imaginative 25		
POSITIVE LANGUAGE	Does not sound believable 0	Arouses doubt 2	Positive 4	Very positive 7	Extremely enthusiastic 10		
EMPHASIS ON IMPORTANT PASSAGES	None 0	Should be reworked 5	Average 10	Good 15	Attracts attention 20		
EGOMETER	100% 'I' 0	More 'I's' 5	More 'You's' 10	'You' dominates 20	100% 'You' 25		

	Difficult to read 0	**Average** 5	**Easy enough** 10	**Easy** 15	**Very easy** 20
READABILITY (short sentences, simple, short words)	Difficult to read / 0	Average / 5	Easy enough / 10	Easy / 15	Very easy / 20
STRUCTURE	Needs re-structuring / 0	Lacks structure / 4	All right / 8	Well structured / 12	Very well structured / 15
PERSONAL ASPECT	Printed (looks anonymous) / 0	Circular / 4	Commercial / 8	Almost personal / 12	Very personal / 15
INTEREST BOOSTERS	None / 0	Lacking / 2	Average / 4	Good / 7	Very frequent / 10
PAGE BREAKS	None / 0	Too few / 1	Average / 2	Good / 3	Perfect / 5
PROOF	None / 0	Too few / 10	Average / 20	Good / 35	Excellent / 50
CONCLUSION	None / 0	Insufficient / 10	Average / 20	Strong / 35	Very strong / 50
GIFT	None / 0	Average but not exploited / 5	Average and exploited / 10	Good / 15	Very well exploited / 20
P.S.	None / 0	Weak / 5	Average / 10	Good / 15	Excellent / 20
NUMBER OF LINES PER PARAGRAPH	More than 12 / 0	10 to 12 / 5	8 to 10 / 10	6 to 8 / 15	Less than 6 / 20
DYNAMISM	Very heavy / 0	Heavy / 5	Average / 10	Moves along / 15	Very dynamic / 25
Conclusion and total out of 1,000:					1,000

You get the idea? It's really so simple, isn't it? When you get to the bottom of a page, cut your text at a critical point, always leaving out some *important* information, which readers can only discover by turning the page. If you arouse your readers' curiosity, they will turn the page and keep on reading!

How do you judge the quality of your letter?

All right, your letter is finished. It looks good, it reads well, it sounds enthusiastic. You're sure it's going to be successful. But before sending it to the printer, don't you think it would be a good idea to verify each point?

The sales letter checklist on the previous page can help you do just that, both for your own letters and for letters written by other people. Just fill it in and add up the score.

One of the best techniques I know consists of exchanging corrections with a colleague. Let me explain.

When you have a new text, send it to your colleague, along with an analysis form which he or she fills out and sends back to you. In return, you do the same whenever your colleague has a new text that needs correcting.

By doing it this way, correcting your text doesn't have to cost you anything.

In the checklist, each element is listed in order of importance and given a label. This makes it easy to compare different versions of a text on the same subject.

One last piece of advice: *rewrite* your texts! Keep trying to improve your score. It's almost *always* possible. And the more experience you have, the faster you'll get great results!

A final piece of advice

Your texts are worth their weight in gold, so it would be a pity not to protect them. Especially since it's so easy. All you have to do is include a copyright symbol: © followed by your name, the name of the place where you work or reside, and the year the text was written, to warn people that you are protecting your property, and that anyone who plagiarises, or simply copies it risks being sued for copyright infringement.

SUMMARY

To hold your readers' interest from the beginning to the end of your letter:

- include regular 'attention-boosters' (questions, news, summaries, riddles, promises etc.).

Improve your text's readability:

- short opening paragraph;
- short sentences;
- paragraphs of not more than six lines;
- lines of text composed of between 50 and 80 characters;
- short (one or two syllables) and simple words;
- underline important words or phrases;
- different formatting (flush right or left) for important paragraphs;
- transition – springboard words;
- different typefaces (preferably with serif);

Protect your texts.

CHAPTER 12

Order forms, envelopes and follow-ups – all the secrets you need to know

Your presentation so far is perfect. You've come up with:

- an excellent headline;
- a strong postscript (P.S.);
- a captivating first paragraph;
- a letter that holds your readers' interest and keeps them turning pages;
- a conclusion that incites them to act.

Now comes the last link in the chain and it is *tremendously* important!

How to make your order form a success

Golden Rule number 1

- *Never call your order form an 'Order Form'.*

Instead, try to find a kind of headline that creates the impression of a 'soft sell' approach, and of a friendly relationship between you and the prospective buyer.

Here are some examples:

- Free trial period coupon;
- Application for a free 90-day trial period;
- Reservation certificate;
- Cheque for your free gift;
- Coupon for success;

- Subscription coupon for free trial;
- Instant action card;
- Urgent order – send this coupon today.

Golden Rule number 2

- *Make your order form a separate document.*

This document should include:

- a summary of the offer (listing all the advantages readers can expect to gain);
- the price;
- the conditions of the sale:
  (A) exactly what the reader should do;
  (B) exactly what you will do;
- the expiration date;
- the guarantee;
- the free gift;
- the name and address of the prospective client.

Do not leave anything out!

The order form, on its own, should hook prospective clients and convince them to buy. And, most importantly, with just the order form in hand, they should be able to order the product, i.e. they should have all the information they need to do so.

However, be careful of making the opposite mistake: don't ask for too much information. Your aim is to make it as easy as possible for prospects to buy the product. So don't ask for any unnecessary information (which may or may not be useful in future), such as date of birth, telephone number, national insurance number, number of children etc.

Golden Rule number 3

- *Leave enough space! Be clear!*

Design the order form so that there is enough space for the client to write in! There's nothing more annoying than an order form which is very complete and very motivating, which does everything it should, right up to the very last (and most important) moment, where the prospect hesitates because there isn't enough room to fill in his or her name! Writing in tiny letters takes an extra effort and this is precisely what you want to avoid. Remember, make it as easy as possible to fill in the order form! See the following page for an example of a good order form.

Even the Experts Agree that TextBridge OCR for Windows is the Best ...

£99 PLUS P&P & VAT

Why TextBridge over anything else...

- Rated best on fax recognition
- Xerox Palo Alto Research Center (PARC) technology
- Foreign language flexibility
- Recognise directly to Microsoft Word for Windows
- Supports more than 30 scanners

"TextBridge represents extraordinarily good value for money, and succeeds in offering top flight OCR at a rock bottom price."
– Practical PC, October 1993

"The claim by Xerox that TextBridge breaks the OCR price barrier with a £99 Windows product says it all. TextBridge works accurately, is very simple to install and use, and the price is right."
– PC User, August 1993

"...an exceptional OCR package at a remarkably low price."
– Personal Computer Magazine, September 1993

"TextBridge, a new Windows package from Xerox Imaging Systems, offers plenty of accuracy and flexibility but at a knockdown £99."
–Windows User, November 1993

"TextBridge is very simple, offers better than average recognition and is unbelievably cheap."
– Computer Shopper, August 1993
Best Budget Buy

"At £99 it is unbeatable value for money, too."
– Personal Computer World, October 1993

Call now for the local dealer near you
0734 668421

Xerox Imaging Systems, UK Ltd.
Unit 8
Suttons Business Park
READING, RG6 1AZ
Tel.   0734 668421
Fax. 0734 261913

Xerox Imaging Systems
A Xerox Company

YES! I WOULD LIKE MORE INFORMATION ON TEXTBRIDGE.

Name _____
Company _____
Address _____
_____
Post Code _____
Telephone / Fax _____

This advertisement (reduced from A4) is reproduced by permission of Xerox Imaging Systems, UK Ltd, Unit 8, Suttons Business Park, Reading RG6 1AZ.

Golden Rule number 4

■ *Put yourself in the client's shoes.*

Write the text from the client's point of view, as if they were doing the talking.

For example:

'Yes, I'd like to take advantage of your 30-day free trial offer . . .', or

'Please send me _____ at absolutely no risk . . .' etc.

Golden Rule number 5

■ *Make ordering as easy as possible.*

Ideally, all your clients have to do is tick off a couple of boxes: everything is planned in advance. The client's name and address are already on the coupon – there's practically nothing to do!

Extremely important note: Always include a return envelope in your mailing, either:

■ postage paid, or
■ postage to be paid.

It doesn't matter, as long as it's there! If your clients have to start looking around for an envelope or, worse, if they have to go out and buy one, then your chances of making the sale become almost nil.

And, if possible, use a typeface that makes it look like it's typewritten, to give it that personal touch.

Golden Rule number 6

■ *Prepare the groundwork.*

Use the conclusion of your sales letter to direct clients' attention to the order form. Ideally, clients will then move directly from the sales letter to the order form . . .

Golden Rule number 7

■ *Pay attention to the order form's design.*

Finally, and above all, make the order form look official and important.

Also, make sure the information it contains is perfectly consistent with the rest of your mailing (even the most seasoned professional can sometimes overlook some detail, especially if the work of preparing the mailing is spread out over a period of time (How can anyone be expected to recall exactly what they said two weeks before?) and with the type of product you're selling.

If clients notice an inconsistency, they will suspect a trap and decide not to take any chances.

The great secret of an exceptional response – the envelope

Once you know this secret you can increase your returns by 50 per cent.

How? Simply by paying special attention to your outer envelope!

If you were a shopkeeper, your outer envelope would be your window display. This is the *first* means at your disposal to attract the attention of prospective buyers, to identify yourself, and to make people want to come into your shop and look around. There's one factor that works in your favour: it's much easier to open an envelope than the door of a shop. Nevertheless, so many direct mail envelopes are thrown directly into the bin, without even being opened!

So, the primary objective of the outer envelope is to incite the recipient to open it! This is a lot harder than it sounds. However, you have a number of tools at your disposal . . .

Golden Rule number 1

■ *Use messages that work best.*

Attract your prospective buyers' attention!

Some of the classic approaches are to flash a message like this:

- Personal!
- Confidential!
- Free!
- Important!
- Urgent!
- R.S.V.P.
- Please open *immediately*!
- For the addressee only!
- Last chance!
- The favour of a reply is requested

You've seen them all before, but tests show that they are effective!

You can also combine two or more. For example:

- Personal and confidential!
- Urgent, please open immediately!

Golden Rule number 2

■ *Arouse curiosity!*

Once again, you have a number of tools at your disposal to help you attain this objective.

1. Hook people with a promise of gain

'This envelope contains a cheque for £450!'

'How to make money with your scribbling . . .'

2. Write the beginning of an important piece of information on the front of the outer envelope; cut it right in the middle, at the most critical moment and say:

'Continued on the back . . .'

Then do the same thing on the back, saying:

'Continued inside . . .'

3. Ask an intriguing question (or a number of questions) and provide the answers inside . . .

'How much are you worth on today's job market?'

If you use this technique, make sure, whenever possible, that 99.5 per cent of your target clients *cannot* answer the question (or questions) with any precision, otherwise why should they open the envelope?

4. Intrigue people in a more general way

'Discover how 1,000 people found a way to get rid of all their money problems . . .'

The outer envelope is your showcase, but you can also use it to prepare and condition your prospects. Always put a headline on your envelope!

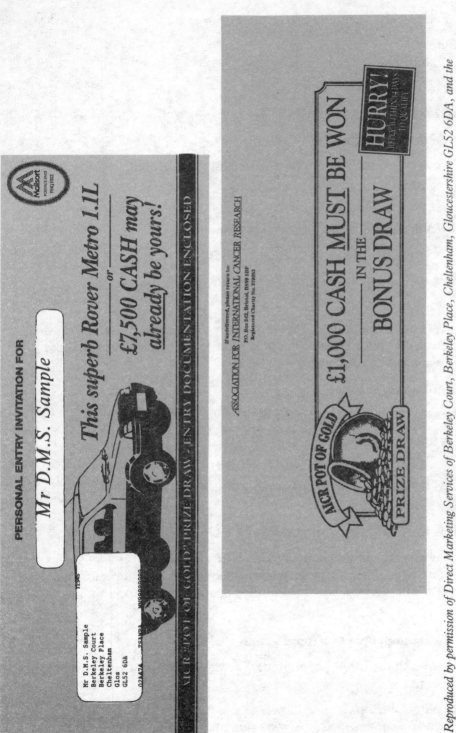

Reproduced by permission of Direct Marketing Services of Berkeley Court, Berkeley Place, Cheltenham, Gloucestershire GL52 6DA, and the Association for International Cancer Research, P.O. Box 242, Bristol BS99 5BF.

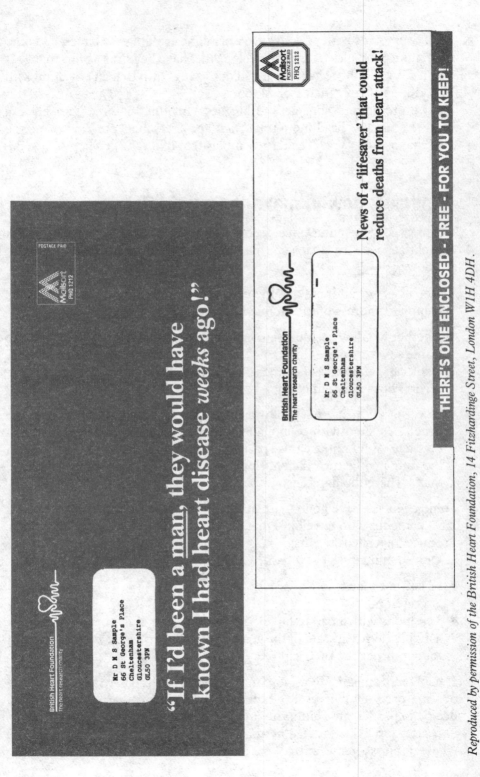

POSTAGE PAID

Mailsort
PHQ 1212

British Heart Foundation
The heart research charity

Mr D M S Sample
66 St George's Place
Cheltenham
Gloucestershire
GL50 3PN

"If I'd been a man, they would have known I had heart disease *weeks ago!*"

Mailsort
POSTAGE PAID
PHQ 1212

British Heart Foundation
The heart research charity

Mr D M S Sample
66 St George's Place
Cheltenham
Gloucestershire
GL50 3PN

News of a 'lifesaver' that could reduce deaths from heart attack!

THERE'S ONE ENCLOSED - FREE - FOR YOU TO KEEP!

Of course, it's better not to have a headline at all than to have a bad one. Also, it's a good idea to test an envelope that has a headline against one that doesn't. But all the tests I've carried out have shown that an envelope with a headline is better than a blank one.

If you're doing a 'business to business' mailing, confine yourself to a more traditional headline ('Important' or 'Personal' etc.) or print the headline using a typeface that resembles that of a typewriter.

Windows: how to make them work for you

I compared your outer envelope to the window display of a shop. This comparison is so true that some mailings use envelopes with more than one window.

- One is for the address, and includes the family and first names, and the complete address of the recipient.

- Another window beside it, either round, triangular or square, is used to frame a picture of a golden coin, for example, or a car or a palm tree etc. Or it can be used as a scratch-to-win box. Some envelopes even have several boxes instead of one.

- One – or a few more – windows on the back of the envelope: these are usually covered with cellophane, and contain a complete promotional message. Why not use this space to best advantage? Ninety per cent of the time people turn the envelope around before opening it – after all, that's where the flap is.

Some agencies have gone to great lengths to develop this technique and have come up with envelopes that are practically transparent. They have produced excellent results.

One such mailing I saw had:

- 17 cut-out tokens (stickers);
- 5 scratch boxes;
- 3 coupons which had to be filled out completely if the person was to be 'eligible' to participate in the games, lotteries, sweepstakes etc., *and*, of course, order the product!

It may seem amazing to want to make people work so hard for a chance to order a product, but in fact experience has shown that people who do decide to participate voluntarily in this series of games, cut-outs, scratchings etc. stop behaving in a normal, rational way – instead, they treat the whole thing as a game, so that, paradoxically, the harder and more exciting it is, the better! In other words, they suspend their disbelief and give themselves over completely to 'the game'.

The game can become a real 'hide and seek' contest between the sender and the recipient, who first reads the front of the envelope, then has to turn to the back, then back to the front and finally back to the back. . . But not really 'finally' because to get the answer, or a piece of the puzzle, or a clue to the riddle, the prospect has to *open* the envelope! And so it goes . . .

To sum up, your envelope should have:

- a window on the front;
- a window on the back.

Some copywriters have even found a way to add a *third window*!

Imagine that you're a prospect and that you've just opened your mailing. To your astonishment, there's nothing in the envelope! Nothing! Really? Most people will make sure by taking a closer look or feeling around inside. And what do they find? Another window, inside the envelope!

Some mailings' envelopes are stuffed full of advertising messages and information. Others just restate the headline directly behind the address window. But more and more mailings use this third window. Remember this when designing your envelope and, if you have the means, do a test!

While we're on the subject, I cannot advise you strongly enough to get your envelopes (both the outer envelope and the return envelope) printed up, and even manufactured completely, if you have the means. This will soon start costing a lot less than working with normal envelopes and your image as a company will benefit enormously. Anything printed is important!

As for the return envelope, having it printed up reassures your prospects and facilitates the transition from passive reader to active buyer. The return envelope should be 'ready to go' – prospects have nothing to do but seal it and drop it in the postbox. Your address is clearly (and correctly) printed and, if possible, the postage is prepaid. All this helps prevent clients from 'putting it off for later. . .' which, as you know, is a sure way to kill a sale.

You can also add things to the return envelope like:

Urgent!

First class post

For the personal attention of:

Even the stamps you use can increase your sales!

Let's talk about stamps.

Franking machines have the advantage of being very fast. Also, you can add your company logo, or a short message, to the space just beside the machine stamp.

But machines have one major fault: they look too official, too impersonal, too cold and unfeeling. The stamps sometimes come out looking dirty – if the machine is not clean it can smudge the ink . . .

That's why many marketing agencies tell their clients to use real stamps and, if possible, a collector's series of stamps (when it isn't too expensive), and *especially* for luxury or costly products.

Some even recommend using more than one stamp. Why? Because stamps are pretty and attractive, brightly coloured, clean and friendly. They clearly add a more personal aspect and, above all, a more important look to your mailing.

Result? Well, depending to some extent on the product, you can expect an average of between 5 and 15 per cent in sales, just because you use a real stamp on your envelope! Pretty amazing, isn't it? Well, let this be a lesson to you: success in direct mail marketing is often due to the know-how and the attention paid to tiny details. They may seem totally insignificant at first glance, but testing has shown that they are extremely effective, and can make all the difference between the success and failure of a campaign.

One last point: if possible, do a test where you send all or part of a mailing from a foreign country. Not only do stamps from other countries add an exotic touch to your mailing, they also make the product more interesting – everything that comes from somewhere else is somehow more appealing and seems more important.

Finally, make sure you respect Post Office rules concerning placement of the address, stamp, return address etc. (See page 162.)

How to double your profits with ease!

Everyone knows about this technique, yet few people make optimum use of it. It really is very simple, once the initial costs (which can be quite high) have been absorbed by the first round of orders. It consists of following up your first mailing with a *second offer*, and it can *double* your returns. Here's how it works:

Say your first mailing costs you £5,000 and resulted in sales of £20,000.

Profit: £20,000 − £5,000 = £15,000

You follow up with a second offer, which costs you £1,000. This brings in 70 per cent of the original sales, or £14,000.

Profit: £14,000 – £1,000 = £13,000

You do a second follow up. Once again, it costs £1,000, but this time it only brings in 50 per cent of the original figure, or £10,000.

Profit: £10,000 – £1,000 = £9,000

Note that after reissuing the product twice, you have already collected £44,000 in total sales, which means a net profit of £37,000, or 2.47 times your initial profit!

You offer the product a third time and get only 40 per cent of your initial sales or £8,000.

Profit: £8,000 – £1,000 = £7,000

Your total profit has risen to **£37,000 + £7,000 = £44,000**, which means that you've more than doubled your initial sales!

These figures demonstrate that it is a good idea to follow up the same product a number of times, instead of making a single offer and then immediately launching a new product, considering all the cost and effort that organising a new mailing involves.

So, the advice is, keep following up the product as long as you keep making money with it!

And, above all, don't worry about annoying your prospective clients. In fact, experience has shown absolutely conclusively that people perceive second, third and fourth offers as proof that the product or service is a good one – in other words, if you take the time and effort to keep writing about it, it must be worth while! So people who were reticent the first time around, and may not have even opened the envelope, will be more curious and more likely to respond to a second or third offer.

Therefore, do not hesitate to follow up your product, two, three, four or even five times!

How to write a follow-up letter

Of course, all follow-up letters should be consistent with what you said before; they should form a 'family' – a cohesive unit. Nevertheless, it's a good idea to vary the style, content and format a little.

For the first follow up, tests have shown that it's best to take exactly the same text that you used for your first mailing, but printed to look like a

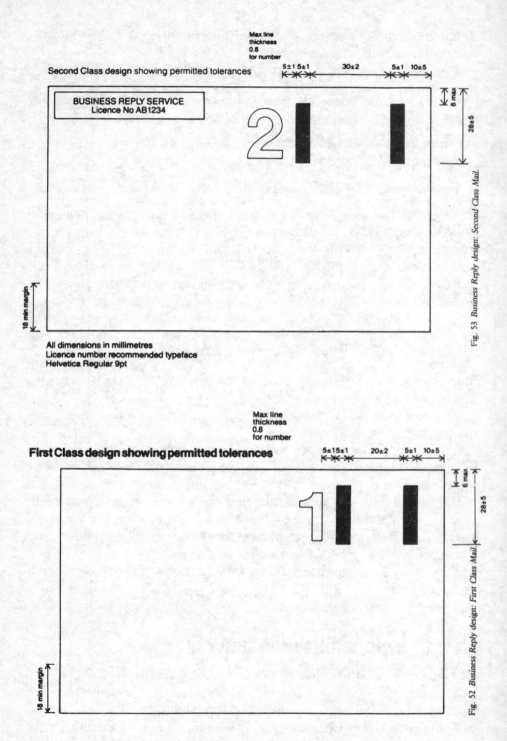

Max line
thickness
0.8
for number

Second Class design showing permitted tolerances

5±1 5±1   30±2   5±1 10±5

BUSINESS REPLY SERVICE
Licence No AB1234

2

6 max

28±5

18 min margin

All dimensions in millimetres
Licence number recommended typeface
Helvetica Regular 9pt

Fig. 53 Business Reply design: Second Class Mail.

Max line
thickness
0.8
for number

First Class design showing permitted tolerances

5±15±1   20±2   5±1 10±5

1

6 max

28±5

18 min margin

Fig. 52 Business Reply design: First Class Mail.

Taken from the Royal Mail Direct Mail Handbook.

facsimile (a carbon copy or photocopy for example), to which you add a handwritten note.

For each subsequent follow up, concentrate on a single argument and develop it further, as follows.

- **Second offer**   Justify the price you're asking.

- **Third offer**   Demonstrate that the product is an investment, which will soon prove to be profitable.

- **Fourth offer**   Emphasise the pride involved in owning the product.

If the product is expensive, offer easier terms of payment in the third or fourth offer. Offer a reduction in price at around the sixth or seventh offer. Be sure to justify the reduction and offer proof: use reasons like minor defects, discontinuing the line, the product minus one of its elements etc.

You should also explain *why* you're writing to the same person again. You could say, for example, that you don't understand the prospect's silence, that you're afraid your first presentation was too short, not clear enough etc.

Another copywriter, Regis Hauser, says in his book, *Conceptualising and Writing Effective Mailings*, that the 'carbon paper follow up' technique has allowed him consistently to add 25 to 55 per cent to his original volume of sales . . . which is far from insignificant! Some companies say that they can generate 75 to 85 per cent more responses by using these follow ups.

He goes on to explain that, on average, sending out:

- the same mailing as the original version results in 20 per cent of the initial responses;

- the same mailing as the original version plus an insert for a 'special last-minute discount' results in between 20 and 45 per cent of the initial responses;

- a different sales letter, which however refers to the first one, and makes the same offer, results in widely varying returns of between 15 and 55 per cent of the initial responses;

- a different sales letter, which makes no reference to the first one, but which offers a discount, also results in widely varying returns of between 35 to 60 per cent of the initial responses;

- a different letter which does not refer to the original, but which offers easier terms, results in about 30 per cent of the initial responses.

Other relevant statistics are as follows.

- Carbon copy follow ups produce 25 to 55 per cent of the initial volume of orders, if expressly written for this purpose.

- Sending out the same mailing a second time: 20 per cent.

- Last-minute discount offer: 20 to 45 per cent.

- A different letter which does not refer to the original: 25 to 55 per cent.

- A different letter *plus* a discount offer: 35 to 60 per cent.

Finally . . . a few more secrets

Here are a few more secret techniques that have been accumulated over years of experience in the field.

Firstly, here are some things that people too often tend to forget when sitting down to write a sales letter.

It takes people a long time to accept a new product. Remember that at first people did not at all take to:

cars;

planes (there's even a brilliant quote by a First World War general who claimed: 'There is absolutely no future in aeroplanes, militarily speaking . . .');

typewriters;

computers; and so on.

We could extend this list to cover a few pages.

Also, absurd rumours and false beliefs can sometimes hinder an already difficult learning process:

- the glue on new stamps was rumoured to contain a poison which caused cancer of the tongue;

- computer screens were said to emit rays which can damage and even destroy the retina. . .

Can you get people to change their habits?

Habits become so embedded in people's minds that they seem to become an integral part of their personalities.

Result: if you ask people to change their habits, you'll find yourself fighting a very powerful force, even if the new habit you're proposing is very advantageous.

So don't try it! It's too risky, and you'll waste too much time and money. Don't even talk about people's 'old habits'. Avoid the subject completely and talk about other things, while always keeping your objective in mind.

On the other hand, make it easy for people to learn new habits that will benefit them (and you!).

There's a subtle line between attacking old habits and creating new ones. The technique, based on applied psychology, has been perfected over years of testing, trial and error – and failure, before being adopted by professional copywriters.

It isn't enough to convince someone that your product is a good one, that it makes sense and is likely to be profitable for that person to buy. Human nature is more complex than that!

In fact, most decisions about whether or not to buy a new product are not based on logic (as you would expect), but on emotion. Why? Quite simply, because people are *afraid* of making decisions.

A few rules about human psychology

If your product is aimed as much at men as it is at women (which is the case with most products), then knowing a few basic rules of human psychology, and especially about the differences between the sexes, can be of enormous help.

Of course, there are exceptions to these rules, but statistically speaking, you will fare a lot better by respecting them.

- Women move more quickly from one idea to another, while men grasp the overall meaning of a sales letter more quickly.

- Men are attracted to verbs, and words which suggest action and dynamism, while women are more impressed by adjectives.

- Women are more interested in people, in others' lives, in social events and in human relations in general than men are (therefore, testimonials work better on women, while men need concrete facts and proof).

- Women are more attracted to colours than men. They're also more sensitive to shades, nuances and subtle tones, while men prefer bright, bold, solid colours.

Back to basics – is your letter logical?

Have you left anything out?

Have you taken care of everything?

I don't want to sound repetitious, but just for the record, are you sure that your letter has:

- a beginning;

- a middle (development phase); and

- a conclusion?

As surprising as it may seem, I often receive sales letters that don't!

Why? Because you can be almost certain that such letters are pasted together, with excerpts taken from other letters, ads, publications etc., instead of being written from scratch. Although laborious enough, this technique is never very effective.

Reading letters like these, you sometimes wonder if there really is any logic to the reasons and arguments being presented in such a seemingly random and disjointed way.

Therefore, it is extremely useful – in fact necessary – when approaching the final phase of writing your own letters, to make sure you get them read and criticised by other people. Always:

- ask other people to read your letters and offer constructive criticism;

- put a letter on the shelf for at least 24 hours, before deciding to use it.

Then read it again from a fresh perspective and ask yourself these questions:

- Is this letter easy to read and to understand?

- Are my thoughts organised into a logical progression?

- Does the letter's style help it flow from one idea to another, and from one argument to the next?

If you have to answer *no* to any of these questions, *rewrite* your letter!

Would you like to improve your style or develop it further?

Just read some of the masters – you can get collected writings and biographies of people like David Ogilvy, Lee Iacocca etc (see bibliography). You don't have to imitate them. Just let their style and logical approach impregnate your mind, and your own writing will soon become clearer, simpler and more easily understood.

A final 'trick'

Some of the great copywriters are so proud of their 'creations' that they have no qualms about reading them out loud to people and discussing them as much as possible.

Why?

- First, because reading a text out loud helps you determine very quickly exactly what 'works' and what doesn't.

- Secondly, because it's the best way to verify that a text has been written in a *conversational* tone – as if you were talking to your prospective clients face to face.

This is one test that never fails . . .

SUMMARY

- Never call your order form an order form.

- Your order form should be a sales document which incites prospects to buy the product all on its own.

- Your outer envelope is both a business card and a display window. Plan it carefully and you'll reap the benefits in higher sales.

- Follow-up mailings can double your profits: always look for ways to exploit this resource to its fullest.

- Don't fight people's habits: it's too risky, and may cost you a lot of wasted time and money. Always lead into something new by referring to something old and familiar.

- Take a step back – let some time go by – and then read your letter again to make sure it's logical and well constructed.

- Read your letter out loud to people and make any necessary changes based on what you detect, and what they say.

. . . .

CHAPTER 13

Troubleshooting and testing

How to give your mailing a sense of unity

When writing your letter, you may find that the information you've pieced together, and the ideas and arguments that have occurred to you, do not come together to form a cohesive whole. In other words, they lack unity.

What can you do?

The trick is to decide on *one dominant idea*. Often linked to the headline, this dominant idea becomes the 'spine' or 'skeleton' that holds all the pieces of your text together.

Of course, you should choose a forceful, original and, if possible, irresistible idea as your central theme. Start by reading over all your arguments and asking yourself this question: 'If there were only one, single reason why a prospect should or should not buy (my product), what would it be? What is my strongest argument?'

Once you've decided what the central idea is, make sure it appears in the different parts of your message, i.e. in all the various elements of your mailing:

outer envelope;

sales letter;

brochure;

lift-letter;

order form.

Then use a tree diagram to list all the other ideas that are connected to this skeletal, central idea:

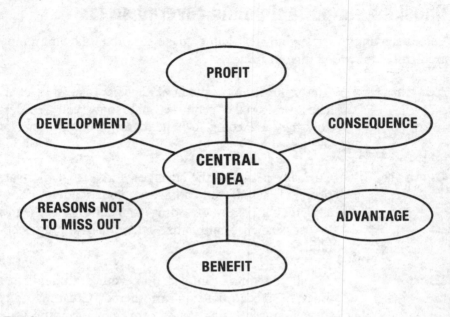

Tree diagram.

The simpler the message, the better it will be understood

When you write, you may refer to information that you assume everyone has access to. But this is not the case. We're all different. Your way of thinking may not be the same as your neighbour's.

Also, when you're trying to get people to accept some kind of new idea, you must simplify it as much as possible and repeat it a number of times.

Someone may read your letter and object. 'But you already said this earlier on!'

Maybe so. But don't forget that a lot of readers 'scan' the pages instead of reading though the text. Contrary to what you may assume, your text will most probably not be read from beginning to end.

Say you have to go out for a while, but you have to get an important message to your wife. How are you going to make sure she gets the message?

It's easy – just put little notes all over the place. She'll be sure to find at least one of them!

If you want to be sure your prospects understand certain ideas, certain key advantages your product has to offer, do the same thing – *repeat* your message by posting it in different places!

Checklist: important points covered so far

Before starting to write your next letter, make sure the following points are firmly embedded in your mind.

Advantages Always speak in terms of *advantages* instead of characteristics. Make promises and show your readers how they are going to benefit from your product or service.

Curiosity Curiosity is one of the strongest forces that motivate people to act. If you can arouse your readers' curiosity, they'll continue reading your letter. Learn how to use suspense and other attention-grabbing techniques.

Unity Tie all your bits of information, your arguments and ideas to a central idea – or theme. Creating unity means concentrating your energy. In the same way, light, when concentrated, can set objects on fire – and even become a weapon.

Assurance People are sceptical. Readers are afraid of being tricked. You know that your offer is serious. Your readers don't know that. Reassure them. Give them proof, references, examples and a foolproof guarantee.

The offer Work on your offer. Make it irresistible. Offer one, or a number of gifts, a rebate, any extra advantages you can think of. Support your offer with good reasons for accepting it. A good offer can make all the difference between failure and a tremendous success.

Conclusion Maybe you think that your prospects are adults, so there's no need to spell out what they have to do to accept your offer and order the product? Well, you're wrong. By listing exactly what they have to do, step by step, you're actually helping them create action-images in their minds which they need in order to direct their conduct: 1. fill out the coupon; 2. slip it in the envelope, along with your payment or credit card number; 3. drop it in the postbox etc.

Hurry We all have so many things to do and so little time! If you don't give people a reason to act quickly – by reminding them of what they stand to lose if they don't act quickly, and what they can gain if they do – then they might not act at all and you lose sales. *Remember later means never.*

Enthusiasm Enthusiasm is the engine that drives all sales. It gives people the conviction to act and can convince even the most sceptical among us. Of course, you have to curb and control your enthusiasm, depending on the type of clientele you're dealing with. But always try to cultivate this essential quality in your writing and use it at least to some degree. Your own enthusiasm will, in turn, provide you with the energy you need to convince others.

After-sales service Making one sale isn't enough. You want to create an ongoing relationship with your clients, you want them to read about your forthcoming products and even wait impatiently for them to appear. To do this, servicing your clients is vital.

Acknowledge receipt of orders, wrap parcels carefully, add a note of thanks, a little extra gift and always respond to complaints; take care of your clients so that they feel comfortable doing business with you.

Don't forget the most important thing and one that should be reflected in your entire mailing:

THE HEADLINE!

Use your headline on:

the outer envelope;

the top of your sales letter;

your order form;

your brochure; and

everywhere you can!

If your letter is long, sprinkle it with various headlines. An effective headline is the one, single element that can assure your success by:

- stopping readers and capturing their attention;

- maintaining and boosting their interest;

- motivating them to ACT!

The crime you must not commit

Forgetting this element has caused the most loss of revenue in the mail order business that I can think of. It is a hidden treasure, and one that must not be ignored:

TESTING

When I say 'test' you may think I'm referring to market studies done on a new product or on a limited segment of the population etc. In fact, I believe testing consists of changing, adding or removing a single and different element, each time you do a mailing.

In other words, you should never send out only a single message during a mailing campaign!

'That's easy to say', you may be thinking, 'but what if I don't have the money to test two or even more messages?'

However, I'm not telling you to change the whole thing – just one, single element.

How to test a single element

You can, for example, test two different headlines on your outer envelope. Or, if you're using an ordinary envelope, with just 'Confidential' or 'Personal' printed on it, then change the headline on your sales letter.

How should you proceed? It's very simple.

You print up two documents, one with the headline you're already using (which you think is the best one) and another with a second headline. You send the headline you're already using to 80 to 85 per cent of your clients, and the new headline to the remaining 15 to 20 per cent.

The ideas is to learn something new every time you do a mailing.

Are you getting fewer orders with your second headline?

Great! You've just learned what *not* to do!

Is the response better with the second headline? Great! You're making progress and you'll be sure to earn more money next time around.

How to identify orders

I use two techniques for recognising which orders correspond to which tests.

1. Order form codes
Ask your printer to add two or three codes to your order form. For example:

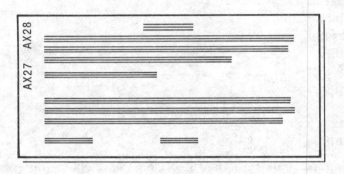

All order forms with these two codes will be classifed as AX28 returns.

Stop the printing when you have enough of these forms and ask the printer to erase the AX28 code from the plate. The remaining order forms will only have the code AX27 on them.

2. The marker
Take a pile of order forms and spread them very slightly to expose the edges, like a pack of cards:

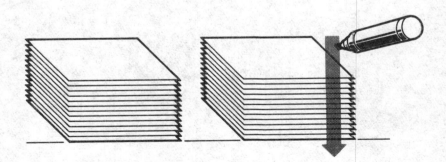

Then use a brightly coloured marker to put a stripe down one side or edge. Use different colours for different tests – it's as easy as that!

SUMMARY

Before printing up the various elements of your mailing, make sure:

- they form a coherent unit;

- you've covered the following nine important points:
  advantages;
  curiosity;
  concentrating your ideas;
  assurance;
  offer;
  conclusion;
  hurry;
  enthusiasm;
  follow up;

- and, of course, most important of all, that each element (outer envelope, sales letter, order form, brochure etc.) displays an effective headline. TEST – TEST – TEST! This is the easiest and surest way to success.

CHAPTER 14

Your future in copywriting and direct sales

Well, that's it! You now know all our little secrets, our tricks and techniques. And now you may be asking yourself the question: 'How is all this going to help me?'

Here are some hints. A direct marketing agency did a study on the number of newspaper ads that had headlines.

The results were surprising: 60 per cent of ads directed at businesses had no headline, no offer, nothing!

And for ads directed at the general public, the figure was even higher – an astounding 80 per cent!

**Conclusion: There's still a great future
out there for good copywriters!**

Whether you're hoping to make big money with a few items that really 'take off', or thinking more about a longer term, smaller profit operation, the difference between success and failure depends on two basic, and closely linked, factors:

- management;

- profits.

Direct marketing has one major advantage over all other types of sales and service sectors: you can start small, with very little money, and by making efficient use of testing and statistics, easily control both your growth rate and your management requirements.

The second big advantage of direct marketing is that it's also possible to develop and increase your profits substantially.

Let me explain: an ordinary business that does not sell by direct mail may show a profit margin of eight per cent. In simple terms, this means that every time the company puts a hundred pounds in the bank, eight of those pounds is profit. To improve this figure, the company could try to reduce production costs, administrative salaries or financial arrangements etc.

These things aren't easy to do. They take a lot of time and a traditional business could only hope to gain one or two per cent added profit anyway. So the best thing they can do is try to increase sales:

> If they were to deposit £150 in sales, their profit would increase to £150 × 8% = £12 profit. However, with only £100, and a profit ratio of, say, 10%, they'd earn £10 profit on every £100.

Result? The head of the company proudly announces higher and higher sales figures, the company expands, new people are hired, new machines are ordered, new offices are decorated etc. Everything gets more and more complicated, cumbersome and difficult to manage.

How to make your profit margin 'take off'

In direct sales, on the other hand, you can easily and rapidly improve your profit margin, without getting bogged down in costly expansion programmes. How? Thanks to good copywriting, of course!

Let's say an initial sales letter resulted in only 0.5 per cent of your addresses actually ordering the product. Still, this covered all your costs (printing, suppliers, postage etc.). For £100 invested, you paid out £99 in costs. Profit ratio: one per cent.

Meanwhile, you've discovered copywriting! You come up with a great headline and an excellent promise; you write a dynamic and captivating letter; a postscript that makes readers *want* to act; your outer envelope arouses curiosity; the order form is very complete and makes ordering so easy . . .

In short, your mailing becomes professional and your returns increase test after test: from 0.5 per cent to two, three, five, seven and even ten per cent.

Let's be conservative and limit ourselves to five per cent: for the same £100 invested, your sales have multiplied ten times!

Result? Your profit margin also multiplies. Say your new approach attains a sales figure of £1,000. This means your new profit margin has jumped from £1,000 minus £99 (costs) = £901. This means you've mutliplied your profit 901 times! And that's exactly what the magic of copywriting can do!

How to become a sought-after copywriter

Sales letters that produce high responses do not happen by accident. Only good copywriters can consistently produce excellent scores. And just reading a book like this one isn't enough to make you a good copywriter.

You are now much more aware of what copywriting is all about. You've been given a host of techniques, professional secrets and basic principles to uphold. That's already a lot! But even today, not many people realise the potential of copywriting and just how powerful a tool it can be.

But, as in all fields, you also have to sweat a little.

Fortunately, the results are well worth the effort!

We know of no other career in the whole world that can give you so much satisfaction (of all kinds) in so short a time . . .

There you have it! A door stands before you. It may lead directly to your personal and professional success. You now know where to find the key. It's up to you to open that door . . .

Good luck!

APPENDIX

About the word 'YOU' – what the experts advise

'How do you go about changing someone's opinion? The most important rule is to start by talking about that person's opinion, and not your own.'

Alain, French Philosopher

'Count the number of times the word "YOU" appears in your text. Talk about your prospects, and not about yourself.'

Drayton Bird

'Make sure that your letter has a logical progression, that it's written in a conversational tone, and that its approach is constantly oriented towards "YOU" rather than "I" . . .'

Nat G. Bodian

'I knew from experience that the word most often used in publicity is "YOU", but I didn't quite realise the extent of its effectiveness . . .'

John Caples

'YOU instead of WE. "We, at the Royal Bank . . ." is an outdated and pedantic turn of phrase, dating back to Victorian times. Rewrite your texts so that they are oriented towards "YOU" instead of "WE".'

Rene Gnam

'Here's one of the great secrets of writing advertising copy: the word YOU. Prospects enjoy being talked about. In fact, they like nothing better!'

Regis Hauser

'Your egotism is what kills your texts and your marketing. More than 90 per cent of the marketing texts I analysed spoke more about the seller than the buyer. To sum up, NEVER, NEVER talk about yourself again. About your interests, your company, your products, your services. From now on, stop being so egotistical!'

Dr Jeffrey Lant

"YOU – YOUR": every mail order ad absolutely must talk about the reader, and involve him or her directly.'

J.P. Lehnish

'The rule of "YOU first" tells readers, listeners and watchers what you can do for THEM, and not what concerns you.'

Hercshell Gordon Lewis

'Continue using the word "YOU" and show your prospects what benefits they will get.'

James E.A. Lumley

'I force myself to write like one person talking to another, in a style that's as direct as possible, using the word YOU . . .'

David Ogilvy

'Make your headline personal by using the magic words "YOU" and "YOURS".'

Kathryn Retzler

'Does your letter have a YOU approach throughout? You can do it. It's easier than you think. All you have to do is put yourself in your client's shoes. As the saying goes, "If you want to sell something to John Jones, you have to see John Jones as if you were John Jones yourself".'

Max Ross

'Use "I" and "YOU" with a majority of You's.'

Joan Throckmorton

'The primordial point of view: the point of YOU . . . We can't emphasise the importance of this point often enough. Forty-three of the best headlines we could find contain at least one of these words: YOU, YOUR, YOURSELF.'

Victor O. Schwab

'Frankly speaking, who do you find the most interesting person in the world? When you pray – if you pray – who are you asking to be blessed? When you judge or criticise someone, are you likely to get more upset if that person offended one of your friends, or if they offended you? If you're with a group of friends, and a fortune teller is predicting the future, whose future are you interested in the most? Are you interested in an analysis of someone else's handwriting, or your own?

'The word "YOU" provokes a universal response in people. Tell me, what word do you think affects us most? What is the most important word we can hear or read? What word makes us respond most quickly?

The incontestable answer is the word YOU.'

Professor W.D. Scott

'Personal pronouns take the prize for effectiveness. They are a substitute for names. We use them in conversation, when we've forgotten the name of the person we're talking to. In such situations, the words "YOU – YOUR – YOURSELF" are constantly being used.'

Professor S. Vogele

Bibliography

Advertising That Pulls Response by Graeme McCorkell (McGraw-Hill)

Benn's Media (Benn Business Information Services Ltd, Tonbridge, Kent)

Better Business Writing by Maryann V Piotrowsky (Piatkus)

Be Your Own PR Expert by Bill Penn (Piatkus)

Common Sense Direct Marketing by Drayton Bird (Kogan Page)

Getting Through to People by J Nirenberg (Prentice-Hall)

Getting to Yes by Roger Fisher and William Ury (Century Business Books)

Glossary of Direct Marketing Terms (DMA)

Guerrilla Marketing Excellence by Jay Conrad Levinson (Piatkus)

High Performance Sales Training by Lee Boyan (Mercury)

How I Raised Myself from Failure to Success in Selling by Frank Bettger (Mandarin)

How to be a Winner by Nick Thornley and Dan Lees (Mercury)

How to Sell Yourself by Joe Girard (Warner Books)

How to Win Friends and Influence People by Dale Carnegie (Mandarin)

Making Direct Response Fund Raising Pay Off: Outstanding Fund Raising Letters and Tips by Jerry Huntsinger (Bonus Books, distributed by Gazelle Book Services)

Maximarketing by Stan Rapp (McGraw-Hill)

My Life in Advertising by Claude Hopkins (National Textbook Company – distributed by Tiptree)

Ogilvy on Advertising by David Ogilvy (Pan Books)

P.R. Planner (Media Information Ltd, London)

Secrets of Closing Sales by Charles B Roth (Prentice-Hall)

Successful Direct Marketing Methods by B Stone (NTC Business Books – distributed by Tiptree)

Success Through a Positive Mental Attitude by Napoleon Hill and W Clement Stone (Thorsons)

The British Code of Advertising Practice (free from the ASA)

The Craft of Copywriting by Alastair Crompton (Hutchinson)

The Handbook of Direct Mail by Siegfried Vogele (Prentice-Hall)

The Joy of Selling by Michael Beer (Mercury)

The Right Brain Manager by Dr Harry Alder (Piatkus)

The Secrets of Effective Direct Mail by John Frazer Robinson (McGraw-Hill)

Write Right by Jan Venolia (Ten Speed Press)

Writing to Sell by Kit Sadgrove (Robert Hale Ltd)

The following books are mentioned in the text, but are not currently available in the UK. They are available in France:

Autobiography of Lee Iacocca (Bantam Books, New York)

Conceptualising and Writing Effective Mailings by Regis Hauser (Ed. d'Organisation, Paris)

Readability by Francois Richardeau (RETZ, Paris)

Secrets of Direct Mail Sales by John P Lehnish (Ed. d'Organisation, Paris)

Useful addresses

Advertising Standards Authority and Committee of Advertising Practice, Brook House, 2–6 Torrington Place, London WC1E 7HN
Tel: 071–580 5555

Advertising Standards Authority for Ireland, IPC House, 35–39 Shelbourne Road, Dublin 4
Tel: 010 353 16 608 766

Data Protection Registrar, Wycliffe House, Water Lane, Wilmslow, Cheshire SK9 5AF
Tel: 0625 535777

Direct Mail Information Service, 5 Carlisle Street, London W1V 5RG
Tel: 071–494 0483

Direct Mail Services Standards Board, 26 Eccleston Street, London SW1W 9PY
Tel: 071–824 8651

The Direct Marketing Association (UK) Limited, Haymarket House, 1 Oxendon Street, London SW1Y 4EE
Tel: 071–321 2525

Direct Selling Association, 29 Floral Street, London WC2E 9DP
Tel: 071–497 1234

Incorporated Society of British Advertisers, 44 Hertford Street, London W1Y 8AE
Tel: 071–499 7502

The List and Database Suppliers Group (contactable through the DMSSB)

Mail Users' Association, Pharos House, Wye Valley Business Park, Hay on Wye, Hereford HR3 5PG
Tel: 0497 821357

Office of Fair Trading, Field House, Bream's Buildings, London EC4A 1PR
Tel: 071–242 2858

Royal Mail Streamline, PO Box 1000, Oxford OX4 5XA
Tel: 0865 780400
Handles Household Delivery Service, Mailsort, Response Services and Packet Post

Trading Standards Office (contact your local council for details)

A personal message from the author

I hope that you enjoyed reading *'How to Write Letters that Sell'*. Now put pen to paper (or fingers to keyboard!) and start making more money through increased sales.

Initially only for my personal use, I designed an automatic headline generator for MAC/PC. If you want to ease your writing process, ask for it by writing to the address below.

If you have any comments or queries, I would be delighted to hear from you. You can write to me directly at the address below:

Christian H. Godefroy,
Post Office Box 42,
CH 1885 Chesières,
Switzerland.

About the Authors

Christian H. Godefroy is a top copywriter, author and training specialist. He is the founder of two direct mail publishing companies which market products to hundreds of thousands of people around the world. His books include *The Complete Time Management System, Confident Speaking, Super Health, Mind Power* and *The Outstanding Negotiator*, all published by Piatkus.

Dominique Glocheux is a management consultant and author of *The Boss Generation* (Dunod). He achieved such tremendous results in his business using Christian Godefroy's techniques that he convinced Christian to write this book. He has enhanced the text with his own business-to-business experience.

Index

Piatkus Business Books

Piatkus Business Books have been created for people who need expert knowledge readily available in a clear and easy-to-follow format. All the books are written by specialists in their field.
  Titles include:

General Management and Business Skills
Beware the Naked Man Who Offers You His Shirt Harvey Mackay
Be Your Own PR Expert: the complete guide to publicity and public relations Bill Penn
Complete Conference Organiser's Handbook, The Robin O'Connor
Complete Time Management System, The Christian H Godefroy and John Clark
Confident Decision Making J Edward Russo and Paul J H Schoemaker
Energy, Factor, The: how to motivate your workforce Art McNeil
Firing On All Cylinders: the quality management system for high-powered corporate performance Jim Clemmer with Barry Sheehy
How to Collect the Money You Are Owed Malcolm Bird
How to Implement Corporate Change John Spencer and Adrian Pruss
Influential Manager, The: how to develop a powerful management style Lee Bryce
Leadership Skills for Every Manager Jim Clemmer and Art McNeil
Lure the Tiger Out of the Mountains: timeless tactics from the East for today's successful manager Gao Yuan
Managing Your Team John Spencer and Adrian Pruss
Outstanding Negotiator, The Christian H Godefroy and Luis Robert
Problem Solving Techniques That Really Work Malcolm Bird
Seven Cultures of Capitalism, The: value systems for creating wealth in Britain, the United States, Germany, France, Japan, Sweden and the Netherlands Charles Hampden-Turner and Fons Trompenaars
Smart Questions for Successful Managers Dorothy Leeds
Strategy of Meetings, The George David Kieffer

Personnel and People Skills

Best Person for the Job, The Malcolm Bird
Dealing with Difficult People Roberta Cava
Problem Employees, how to improve their behaviour and their performance Peter Wylie and Mardy Grothe
Psychological Testing for Managers Dr Stephanie Jones

Financial Planning

Better Money Management Marie Jennings
Great Boom Ahead, The Harry Dent
How to Choose Stockmarket Winners Raymond Caley
Perfectly Legal Tax Loopholes Stephen Courtney

Small Business

How to Run a Part-Time Business Barrie Hawkins
Making Profits: a six-month plan for the small business Malcolm Bird
Profit Through the Post: How to set up and run a successful mail order business Alison Cork

Motivational

Play to Your Strengths Donald O Clifton and Paula Nelson
Winning Edge, The Charles Templeton

Self-Improvement

Brain Power: the 12-week mental training programme Marilyn vos Savant and Leonore Fleischer
Creating Abundance Andrew Ferguson
Creative Thinking Michael LeBoeuf
Memory Booster: easy techniques for rapid learning and a better memory Robert W Finkel
Organise Yourself Ronni Eisenberg with Kate Kelly
Quantum Learning: unleash the genius within you Bobbi DePorter with Mike Hernacki
Right Brain Manager, The: how to use the power of your mind to achieve personal and professional success Dr Harry Alder
Three Minute Meditator, The David Harp with Nina Feldman

Sales and Customer Services

Art of the Hard Sell, The Robert L Shook
Creating Customers David H Bangs
Guerrilla Marketing Excellence Jay Conrad Levinson
How to Close Every Sale Joe Girard

How to Make Your Fortune Through Network Marketing John Bremner
How to Succeed in Network Marketing Leonard Hawkins
How to Win Customers and Keep Them for Life Michael LeBoeuf
Sales Power: the Silva mind method for sales professionals José Silva and Ed Bernd Jr
Selling Edge, The Patrick Forsyth
Telephone Selling Techniques That Really Work Bill Good
Winning New Business: a practical guide to successful sales presentations Dr David Lewis

Presentation and Communication
Better Business Writing Maryann V Piotrowski
Complete Book of Business Etiquette, The Lynne Brennan and David Block
Confident Conversation Dr Lillian Glass
Confident Speaking: how to communicate effectively using the Power Talk System Christian H Godefroy and Stephanie Barrat
He Says, She Says: closing the communication gap between the sexes Dr Lillian Glass
Personal Power Philippa Davies
Powerspeak: the complete guide to public speaking and presentation Dorothy Leeds
Presenting Yourself: a personal image guide for men Mary Spillane
Presenting Yourself: a personal image guide for women Mary Spillane
Say What You Mean and Get What You Want George R. Walther
Your Total Image Philippa Davies

For a free brochure with further information on our range of business titles,
please write to:

Piatkus Books
Freepost 7 (WD 4505)
London W1E 4EZ

PIATKUS